FEEL SOMETHING, MAKE SOMETHING

WRITTEN & ILLUSTRATED
BY CAITLIN METZ

FEEL SOMETHING, MAKE SOMETHING

a GUIDE To COLLABORATING WITH YOUR EMOTIONS

Clarkson Potter/Publishers
New York

Published in the United States by Clarkson Potter/Publishers, an imprint
of Random House, a division of Penguin Random House LLC, New York.

clarksonpotter.com

CLARKSON POTTER is a trademark and POTTER with colophon is a
registered trademark of Penguin Random House LLC.

Library of Congress Cataloging-in-Publication Data has been applied for.

ISBN 978-0-593-23494-5

Ebook ISBN 978-0-593-23495-2

Printed in China

Design by Caitlin Metz and Danielle Deschenes

10 9 8 7 6 5 4 3 2 1

First Edition

for Charlie

Charlie, 16.5 months
2022

CONTENTS

Intro (pg. 11)

A lil' narrative about what art-making has meant to me over the years. Bring your tissues, it's a real sweet love story.

Part One: The Feeling (pg. 30)

In this section of the book, I share my two favorite practices for getting in touch with my feelings. First, I use bodymaps (pg. 42) to visualize the sensations within my physical form. Then I empty my thoughts onto the page, creating a mindmap (pg. 54) to make sense of what's happening in my head. These exercises provide space between me and the *Feel* so that I may investigate it fully.

Part Two: The Making (pg. 67)

Once you know what you're feeling, it's time to make something about or with it. In this section, I give you a pep talk about creating within the constraints of your everyday life. Then I wax poetic about five functions of art-making that have guided my practice, plus the artists I'm in awe of. And finally, I share how to make a studio wherever you are (pg. 110) and offer up some tutorials of my favorite things to create (pg. 118).

THIS
FLUFFY BIT
GETS ME
EVERY TIME

INTRO

IN WHICH I TELL YOU A BIT
ABOUT WHAT MAKING THINGS
MEANS TO ME

I spend my days documenting the sky, my body, and the thoughts filling my head. Half-finished poems litter my notes app in strange configurations that often don't make sense . . . until suddenly they do. I don't question how the wisp of a cloud sends me running to the rooftop balcony, or why I must draw the way fear eats away at my belly. Sometimes it takes months or years for patterns to emerge between all my practices. A trail of clues; secrets not yet revealed. An intimate collaboration between me and the universe.

I hope these pages spark your very own practice of listening and responding to the surges of desire and oceans of emotion within you.

Here we embark on the magnificent sequence, old as time herself: Feel something, make something. Rinse and repeat.

This book is about release: releasing your tangled thoughts and tenderest emotions through the act of art-making. It's about letting it all out onto paper so you can make sense of your feelings from some distance. It's the alchemy of transmuting emotion into artifacts. This work allows you to hold the inexplicable in your hands, run your fingers across the spine of longing, crumple grief in your fist, or pin your rage to the wall so you can step back, take a breath, and examine the contents of your heart and mind from a fresh point of view.

When I create from my feelings, the enigmatic becomes manifest; mark-making reverberates like an echo delineating the edges of my consciousness, a mirror reflecting the inconceivable. Something transcendent happens when we allow the swirling, fearsome tangle to tumble out onto paper, canvas, or clay or into poetry, song, or dance.

This process—this aching, messy, broken, perfect process of scribbling thought and feeling onto paper—is the work. It's everyday magic. And it's available to us at a moment's notice.

So where do we begin? The hardest part for me is pausing to listen. In a lot of ways, knowing when to make something is a chicken-and-egg situation. I know it's time to create when I feel overwhelmed, tired, irritable, anxious, etc. But I'm so good at pushing past my feelings that I often don't realize I'm having them until I pause ... and for me the pause comes when I make something. So as you can see, sometimes you have to start before you know where to begin.

I sharpen my sensitivity to the quiet whispers of my body and mind every time I create work in collaboration with the feelings and sensations resonating inside.

There's a beautiful quote attributed to Viktor E. Frankl about the power of listening/noticing: "Between stimulus and response there is a space. In that space is our power to choose our response. In our response lies our growth and our freedom."

The simple act of picking up a pencil stretches that liminal space of feeling into a place of rest where I can explore all manner of possible responses.

MORE FEELING, ←—MY MOTTO
LESS REACTING

Over the years, I've found myself repeating the same patterns when processing my emotions. The practices I'm sharing here are the ones I've turned to intuitively over the past two decades—my sanctuary when leaving religion, the voice I borrowed to whisper my way out of the closet, a healing balm to soothe C-PTSD.

As long as I can remember, drawing has been my refuge. I leave the ache of this world, everything goes still, and the only thing that matters is the line on a page. I would draw for hours and hours as a child. Copy paper on top of a book balanced on my knees, Mead mechanical pencil in my left hand, eraser crumbles littering the couch cushions around me.

My favorite thing to draw was women: with endless piles of hair and unimaginably tiny waists, wearing Victorian-era dresses with lots of flounces. Secretly I'd draw them naked first, huddled in a corner so no one could see, quickly drawing a dress over the curves that made me feel warm in ways I didn't yet understand. SWEET TENDER BABY QUEER CAITLIN THIS BOOK IS FOR YOU. ♡

Drawing—or mark-making—has been a space for me to explore concepts without committing—before language, there were images. (I like to say "mark-making" over "drawing" because it softens the idea of drawing as a rigid, specific type of skill. Anyone can make a mark!) Mark-making allows my body to speak about things for which there are no words. Illustrating my anxiety gave me language to ask for help. Repetitive lines introduced me to meditation. Notes scrawled on bar napkins became life-affirming manifestos.

When I was sixteen, I took a series of photos of myself crying. I edited them in rich pinks and purples to try and capture the crushing teenage loneliness and despair (you know the one), those waves of emotion that leave you gasping for air. I thought I'd implode if I didn't let it all out. So I started photographing myself as a means of release. Those images validated my experience. I captured singular moments of pain and gave each one a place to rest. This made room to acknowledge the presence of pain without being consumed by it. I didn't have words for any of this at the time. I didn't understand the need to bear witness to myself in this way. It felt self-indulgent. Now I understand it as self-preservation.

Fast-forward to my mid-twenties, halfway through grad school. I've finally come out as queer, ~~but~~ AND I'm engaged to be married (to a man). I'm breaking out of fundamentalist evangelicalism—for good this time. I'm admitting to my debilitating anxiety and depression. Nothing makes any sense. In a frantic panic after too many days spent curled in the fetal position, crying on the floor under my studio table, I began the simple practice of drawing myself every day for 100 days (inspired by Elle Luna's 100-Day Project—a community commitment to making something for 100 days in a row).

What came from that daily practice was a collection of 100 absurd, each-different-from-the-one-before portraits, drawn without lifting my pen or looking down at my paper. It was an acceptance of the tension within me. Through these blind contour drawings, I was able to see myself. All my selves. And for the first time they didn't contradict one another, or maybe there was finally space for all the difference.

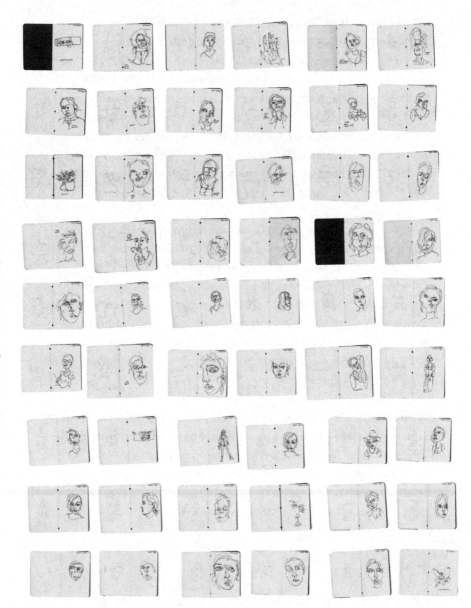

18

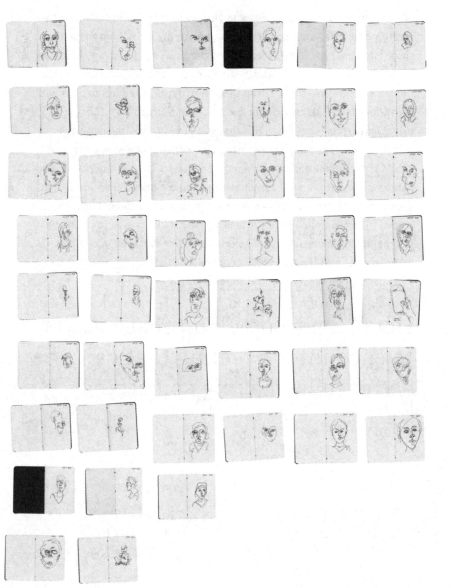

Most recently, I turned to drawing in that save-my-life kind of way while creating and sustaining an entire human with my body. From the moment those two pink lines showed up, drawing took on a gravity that anchored me like never before. In the thirty-nine weeks and one day I spent in the liminal state of pregnancy, I drew every horrifying sensation to cope with the terror I felt (making a person didn't come easily to me). Then, in those early postpartum days, when the shadows got long and the darkness crept in like a soul-sucking dementor, I'd balance that wee eight-pound tangle of limbs between two aching breasts and race ahead of the chilling panic, one line at a time. These drawings found a home on an Instagram page dedicated to the operation of growing this tiny human. Messages poured in at odd hours, as night-feeding parents from around the globe sought comfort alongside me. The echoes of "me too" and "you're not alone" punctuated the night like a constellation. And once again, mark-making gave me direction in the midst of chaos.

Here I am to proclaim that I've yet to encounter a feeling that can't be softened by making something.

WE SPENT THE FIRST
THREE MONTHS
JUST LIKE THIS

Charlie, 16.5 months
2022

It often seems like my feelings have feelings. The core feel is like a stone thrown into a pond, with all the subsequent feels rippling out. Art-making slows things down so I can differentiate the pebble from the rings and keep my thoughts from spiraling into spaghetti soup.

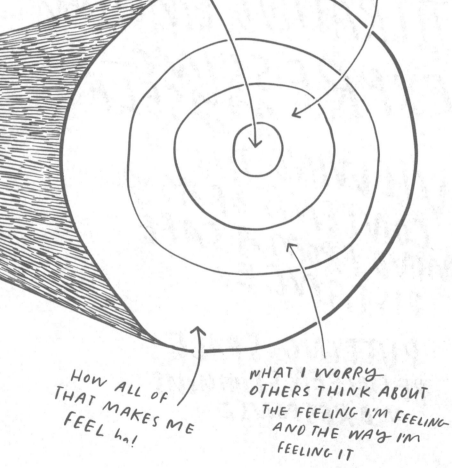

the FEELING

HOW I FEEL ABOUT
THE FEELING

HOW ALL OF
THAT MAKES ME
FEEL ha!

WHAT I WORRY
OTHERS THINK ABOUT
THE FEELING I'M FEELING
AND THE WAY I'M
FEELING IT

25

Here are a few of the ways art-making has supported me through the years . . .

TITRATING EMOTION

EXPRESSING MYSELF

VIEWING THE CONTENTS OF MY MIND FROM A SAFE DISTANCE

PUTTING SPACE BETWEEN STIMULUS AND RESPONSE

BRINGING THOUGHTS INTO FOCUS

SELF-REGULATING and SELF-SOOTHING

SPEAKING UP FOR SOMETHING THAT I BELIEVE IN

HAVING A CONVERSATION WITH MYSELF

I've discovered five distinct functions for self-preservation within art-making: ritual, documentation, conversation, expression, and disruption. Depending on my need, these modes of creation offer me comfort, clarity, and direction; it's where I lay my burdens down. Art-making is a vast landscape, offering us all a place to nestle in and rest. It's in this container of creation that I find myself, over and over again.

MARK-MAKING HAS
BEEN SAVING MY LIFE
SINCE I WAS OLD ENOUGH
TO HOLD A CRAYON.

IT IS MY WAR CRY
AND SALVE;

I HOPE IT WILL
BE FOR YOU TOO.

PART ONE
THE FEELING

IT'S
BEEN
A WHILE
SINCE I'VE
SAT WITH
MYSELF

Oct 14

Cheerios
Toasted whole oat fresh Cereal!

made with 100% WHOLE GRAIN OATS

Gluten-free

NET WEIGHT 12 oz (340g)

STRAIGHT BOURBON WHISKEY

COMFORT FOOD
TO SOOTH̶ THE
  ^soothe
STING OF REJECTION

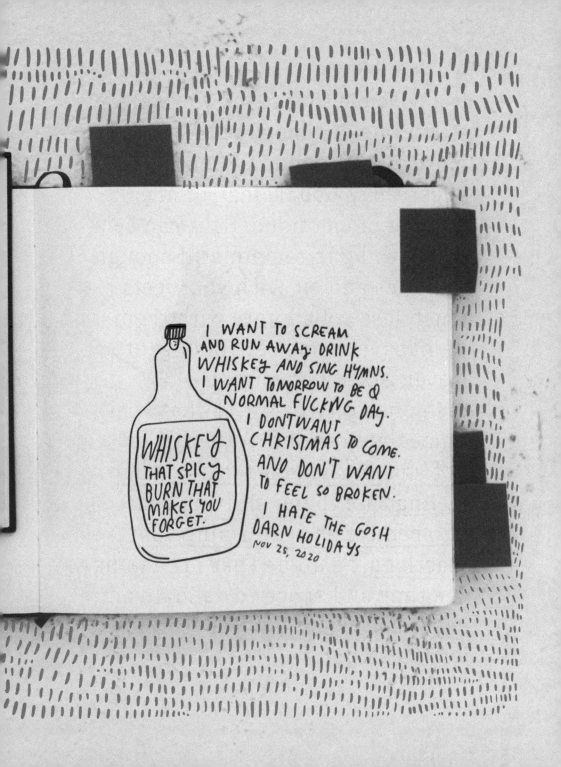

I WANT TO SCREAM
AND RUN AWAY. DRINK
WHISKEY AND SING HYMNS.
I WANT TOMORROW TO BE Q
NORMAL FUCKING DAY.
I DON'T WANT
CHRISTMAS TO COME.
AND DON'T WANT
TO FEEL SO BROKEN.
I HATE THE GOSH
DARN HOLIDAYS
NOV 25, 2020

WHISKEY
THAT SPICY
BURN THAT
MAKES YOU
FORGET.

It's possible that since you were a tiny human you were taught to move away from or against grief, anger, envy, doubt, fear, or any number of emotions. So it can be a whole thing to remain still enough to notice and sit with your feels, much less collaborate with them. Perhaps it seems self-indulgent. Navel-gazey. Like a good old-fashioned pity party. To that I call immediate bullshit. Whether or not you're paying attention, your feelings are there, shifting your perspective and informing your reactions. I'd argue that not taking the time and space to validate and experience what you are feeling is what's selfish. ☺ *BLOOP!*

DO YOU FEEL LIKE IT'S WEAK, SELF-ABSORBED, ETC., TO SPEND TIME WITH YOUR FEELINGS?

WHERE DID THIS STORY COME FROM? (WHERE AND HOW IS IT REINFORCED?)

PARENTS? MEDIA? PATRIARCHY? FEAR OF REJECTION? SCHOOL? SOCIETY? CULTURAL NORMS? RELIGION?

WHAT EMOTIONS FEEL THE MOST DIFFICULT TO SIT WITH OR ACCESS? WHICH DO YOU FEEL THE NEED TO HIDE?

WHICH COME EASILY?

DO YOU HAVE A FAVORITE EMOTION/SENSATION/FEELING?

Some of the ways my body lets me know that I'm having a feel.

Isn't it wild how a lot of these sensations show up for both positive and negative feelings? Can you keep track of how often you feel the same kind of physical sensation in different sorts of emotional situations?

FROZEN— CAN'T MOVE or FEEL your BODY

OVERWHELMED BY CHOICES

OUT of CONTROL

IMPATIENT, ANXIOUS, MANIC SENSATIONS or IMPULSES

SHALLOW BREATHING

SPINNING THOUGHTS CAN'T FOCUS ON ANYTHING

IN a HAZE or FOG

a SUDDEN URGE To HIDE or REPRESS an EMOTION

SUDDENLY HEIGHTENED or LOWERED INHIBITIONS

SURGE of ADRENALINE or ENERGY

My top avoidant strategies. Zero out of ten, would not recommend.

What tactics do you use to avoid uncomfortable sensations and emotions? What are the side effects of evading yourself?
(No judgment here, we're just getting curious!)

NETFLIX BUT NO CHILL

RED WINE

NUMBING OUT

MIDDLE of THE NIGHT ONLINE SHOPPING

BUY WITH ONE CLICK

HIDING IN BED

DEADLINES

THE SCROLL

OVER-COMMITTING MYSELF

A few of the ways I invite my body to pause and feel the feels.

What practices help you listen to and be present with yourself? When do you feel safest in your body? Think about the things, places, and activities that bring stillness.

WATCHING THE CLOUDS

CONNECTING TO MY SENSES

TAROT DECK

SELF-INQUIRY

WALKING (WITHOUT MY PHONE) — so hard so good

BODYMAPS and MINDMAPS

FEELING your FEELS
CAN BE OVERWHELMING
and EVEN A LITTLE SCARY.
I'VE FOUND Two PRACTICES
TO BE QUITE CONVINCING
WHEN TRYING TO COAX
OUT THE FEELS

LET'S DIVE IN →

These are my favorite tools for excavating feelings. They function as <u>proactive practices</u> when added to your daily rituals, or as <u>emergency self-soothing</u> in moments of panic or overwhelm.

All you need is something to make marks with and something to make marks on: a sticky note and crayon, some chalk and cement, the back of a parking ticket and a Sharpie, or your favorite notebook and pen (what luxury!).

BODYMAP *(the noticing)*

A visceral practice of observing sensations in your body and assigning them words, colors, textures, or objects; correlating the intangible with common imagery, offering context and a gentle entry into the ancient wisdom of our bodies.

MINDMAP *(the processing)*

A cerebral practice of emptying the contents of your mind onto paper in pursuit of making connections between concepts and ideas; providing a safe container to explore the tangled thoughts and feelings swirling around your mind.

Bodymaps are the way I pause and listen to myself; it's how I know where to begin. Without them I find it much harder to know how I feel or what I need. I scan my body, breathe deeply, and get curious about every single sensation between the top of my head and the very bottom of my feet. Then I take notes: I like to label my discoveries with colors, textures, scribbles, objects, animals, and shapes. This gives a tangible representation to the often abstract feelings within.

I love this particular exercise for moments of panic or overwhelm because it requires taking on the role of an observer, immediately making space between me and the sensations in my body. I don't have to rationalize or shift anything, just make a corresponding mark to where I'm feeling a thing. It also brings me back to myself when I'm dissociated or numb by gently inviting me to notice sensation again.

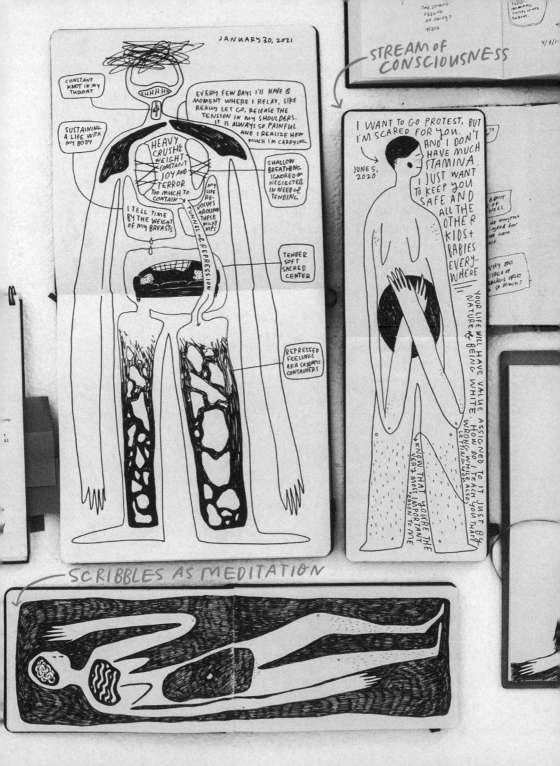

Right now, as I'm writing this, there is a weird ache behind my left ear, my eyes feel heavy, warm tea lingers in my throat, and my arms ache. I just handed baby Charlie off to my partner, and it usually takes me a minute to relax the muscles that are perpetually engaged to hold, rock, sway, and comfort. Once I let them release, I feel such a weight: heavy, exhausted, relieved ... and then empty, longing, tired so tired, and missing that little squish. My mind feels a little fuzzy. I'm trying to focus on these words, but it's spinning in a million directions.

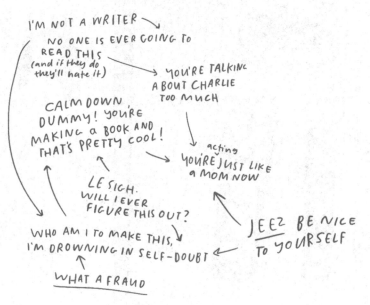

My neck is stiff from balancing my computer on my knees while wrangling my tiny human into feeding positions all morning. My chest feels heavy, like there is a rock on my lungs, crushing into my heart, I can feel myself pushing the feelings down. Way down into my legs. Away from consciousness. My soft belly is tender, where I hold my heart these days, like a favorite worn-in couch.

My arms wrap around my waist, my core, warm and radiating, reminding me that the tiny being it grew into still needs me close. Legs. If I think about them for a bit, I feel tingles, tiny twinges that let me know they're still attached to my body. I sometimes completely neglect to wash the lower half of my body in the shower because I forget it's even there. What even are legs but sadness containers? I've been trying to remember that I have form beyond my waist. It's a work in process.

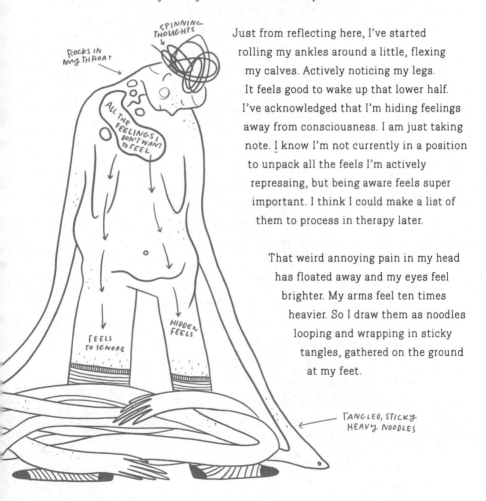

Just from reflecting here, I've started rolling my ankles around a little, flexing my calves. Actively noticing my legs. It feels good to wake up that lower half. I've acknowledged that I'm hiding feelings away from consciousness. I am just taking note. I know I'm not currently in a position to unpack all the feels I'm actively repressing, but being aware feels super important. I think I could make a list of them to process in therapy later.

That weird annoying pain in my head has floated away and my eyes feel brighter. My arms feel ten times heavier. So I draw them as noodles looping and wrapping in sticky tangles, gathered on the ground at my feet.

HOW TO MAKE A BODYMAP

OUTLINE YOUR BODY

There's no magic here, just a line making the form of a body; a head, torso, and limbs. Don't get stuck on making it perfect. All you need is a frame to hold what you're feeling. Sometimes my bodymaps are tight and realistic, other times they have more in common with a blob than a person. Let it be playful, make a stick person for all I care.

ASSIGN WORDS & IMAGES

Take a deep breath and check in with your body. It often helps to start at your head and work down (or vice versa), taking note of what you feel. Can you attach a shape, color, animal, object, texture, phrase, or word to each physical sensation? It doesn't have to make sense. Just listen to everything your body is telling you, and mark it down on the corresponding spot on your outline. This can be a rapid scribble expressing a specific tingle in your body, or you can spend an hour chronicling each and every twinge, ache, longing, and memory lodged inside you. Let this practice be whatever you need it to be.

THAT'S ALL FOLKS

That's all there is to it. This simple practice has taught me so much about the wisdom and creativity of my body. Bodymaps have helped me identify recurring sensations (like how I always shove things I don't want to think/feel down into my legs) and have shown me the warning signs of overwhelm, panic, longing, and anger, so I'm able to attend to my needs before they take over. They've also shown me where peace and relief live in my body, what pleasure and joy feel like, so I can reach out greedily for more. Your body is a book, and it has so much to tell you. Listen, be curious, let it know you're here to collaborate.

LABEL EVERY PHYSICAL SENSATION
YOU'RE EXPERIENCING

LABEL EVERY EMOTION THAT IS
PRESENT FOR YOU AND WHERE
THEY LIVE IN YOUR BODY

MARK ALL THE PLACES YOU
FEEL JOY IN YOUR BODY   OR ANY OTHER
                            EMOTION

MARK ALL THE PLACES YOU
FEEL GRIEF IN YOUR BODY

DRAW ALL THE THINGS
YOU CONSUMED TODAY

I LOVE DOING   (MEDIA, INFORMATION,
THIS ONE →   NOURISHMENT, IDEAS)

GO TO A DISTINCT MEMORY,
SETTLE INTO YOUR BODY, AND MAP
THE SENSATIONS, THOUGHTS, AND
FEELINGS YOU EXPERIENCED AT
THAT TIME

A long but inexhaustive list
of adjectives, in an attempt to
scratch the surface of all the
sensations your body contains . . .

ACHING ACTIVATED BLOATED
BOUNCING BRIGHT BUBBLY
BULBOUS BUMPY BURNING
BUTTERY BUZZING COLD CONCRETE
CONSTRICTED CRUNCHY DANK
ECHOING ELECTRIC EMPTY
EXPLOSIVE EXPOSED FEATHERY
FLAT FLOOFY FLUID FLUTTERY
FOGGY FRAZZLED FRESH FRISKY
FROZEN FULL FUZZY GAPING
GOOEY GRAVELLY GRITTY
GUMMY HARD HEAVY
ITCHY JELLY LANGUID

LIGHT LOUD NEEDLY NOODLY NUMB OPEN PERKY PESKY PLUMP POKEY POOFY PRICKLY RADIATING RELAXED ROCKY ROLLING ROUGH SALTY SANDY SCALY SCRATCHY SHARP SILKY SLEEK SLIMY SMOOSHED SMOOTH SOFT SOGGY SPARKLING SPICY SPIRALING SQUISHY STALE STEADY STINKY STRAIGHT STRETCHED STURDY SUPPLE SWEATY TANGLED TENDER TENSE THIN TICKLISH TORN TRAPPED UNEASY VIBRATING WARM WARPED WATERY WOODEN WOOLLY

Reference this collection of words if you feel stuck, maybe try a few on.
Do you ever feel electric? Stretched? What words resonate deepest in you?
Where do you feel them? Which are recurring? Build your own vocabulary.
Your body has a language all its own.

While you're building up your vocabulary around your feelings, here are some resources for expanding your emotional literacy.

In *Atlas of the Heart*, Brené Brown breaks down eighty-seven different emotions. It's a textbook for life, in my opinion. And of course, the feeling wheel, created by Gloria Willcox is an amazing resource for narrowing in on the root of your feeling by understanding how they might be radiating out from core emotions.

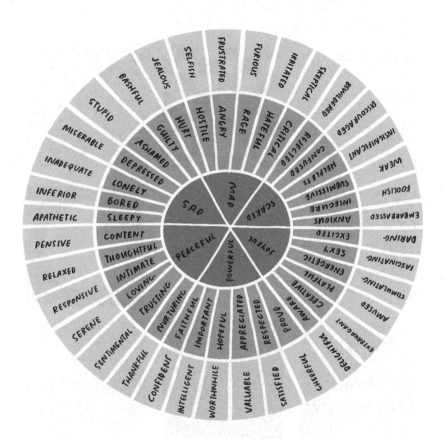

the FEELING
WHEEL *BY GLORIA WILLCOX*

You might also want to create a visual vocabulary for yourself.

What marks are the most satisfying to make when you're angry? What feels soothing? Which ones make you happiest? Which do you find most visually appealing? How many different kinds of marks can you make? Build up your repertoire of emotive gestures to call on when you need something to represent your feelings.

Mindmaps are a web of every thought connected to a central idea. A mindmap is just a fancy word for writing down every thought associated with _____ .

FILL IN THE BLANK

Know when your mind feels like a crayon scribble of sticky spaghetti, blurring your ability to follow a thought? That's when I know it's time to make a mindmap. Take that tangled mess and put it on paper. It takes some getting used to—releasing your thoughts on a page without censoring yourself feels awkward and messy at first, but this practice soothes that white-hot blur in your mind and lets you follow the trails.

IT HELPS UNTANGLE THE OVERCOOKED NOODLY THOUGHTS

THIS IS A CLASSIC MINDMAP

THIS IS JUST STREAM OF CONSCIOUSNESS

fig.1

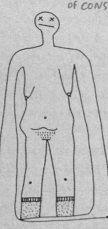

ME TRYING TO NOT BE ANGRY WITH MY PARTNER FOR SLEEPING IN EVERYDAY WHILE I TRY AND BALANCE WORK AND TENDING TO OUR CHILD. I WANT TO SCREAM "THIS IS NOT A VACATION" IN HIS STUPID FACE. INSTEAD I'M SHOVING THOSE FEELINGS INTO MY ARMS. DOWN, DOWN, DOWN INTO THE LONG NOODLES THEY HAVE BECOME. I ALSO FEEL SO GUILTY FOR WORKING AND LEAVING THE BABE WITH HIM. AM I A BAD PARENT FOR LIKING MY WORK? AND ALSO, WTF I'M PAYING ALL OUR BILLS. CAN I NOT MAKE MONEY JOYFULLY? MUST IT ALWAYS HOLD SUFFERING TO BE VALID?

HOW AM I FEELING

SOME DIAGRAMS

ANTIDOTES
SOOTHING
AGENTS
HEALING

INCOMPLETE COLLECTIVES

LISTS!

WILL
NEVER

For the past five years I've been moonlighting as an adjunct professor in the Design and Visual Art program at Maryville University. On the first day of class every semester I write a word on the whiteboard—like "blue"—and coax my new students to the board with shiny new dry erase markers and ask them to write down everything they associate with that color. First, they'll write water, sky, baby boy. Then they look at me expectantly, waiting for the next step. I ask them to keep going. Rain, shower, tub, yellow duck. "Can I put 'yellow duck'?" someone asks. "Is that too far-fetched?" I say there are no rules and ask them to keep going.

There's usually an awkward pause where they're trying to decide if I'm for real. I ask them to think about emotions, places, personal experiences, pop culture, etc. Anything they think of when they read the word "blue." After a painful pause in which no one wants to be the one to write the wrong thing, some awkward student without much to lose will scrawl "the teddy bear from when I was a baby." I say, "Yes! Exactly! Keep going." Someone nervous-laughs and writes Cookie Monster, Sesame Street, Saturday morning, cartoons, cereal. I bounce up and down on my toes and clap. They share a look with their peers and decide I'm both for real and a little kooky, but now they're giggling and writing references to niche memes, video games, and viral TikToks that I know nothing about, and suddenly I feel very old. Someone inevitably gets political. They eye me nervously. I say, "Keep going."

We don't stop until the board is full. <u>It's irreverent, silly; some of it makes</u> <u>sense and lots of it doesn't.</u> All bets are off. Together we write down every association we have to the word "blue." Then I ask them to step back and read the mass of words, to follow the lines between them.

How did we get here? Can you connect central ideas? If we want to remain centered on our initial word, which ideas are hyperspecific to one person, which associations do we collectively agree upon? Do you observe any related concepts we could take note of? The point of this exercise has nothing to do with the word at the center of the whiteboard. It's all about teaching students how to follow a thought. To not censor themselves. To just write down the next idea without judgment.

For every project I assign in class, my students' first job is to mindmap. The magic of this practice is its framework. It gives you space to follow a thought, while slowing your mind down to the rate at which you can translate it onto the page.

THIS IS YOUR JOB TOO.
EVERY TIME YOU'RE FACED
WITH A BIG FEELING, IDEA,
OR NAGGING THOUGHT, FOLLOW
IT THROUGH LIKE THIS TO
UNCOVER WHAT'S UNDERNEATH

1 FEEL SOMETHING
2 WRITE IT ALL DOWN
3 CONNECTIONS + DISCOVERY
4 ORDER + ASSIMILATION
5 MAKE SOMETHING

WE'LL GO OVER EACH OF THESE
STEPS IN THE NEXT PAGES

LET IT ALL OUT

Take that tangle out of your mind and let it spill onto the paper.
Follow each rabbit trail, thought pattern, association, and connection.

In a classic mindmap or word-web, I write a central theme in the middle
of the page. Then, I fill the paper with everything that comes to mind
when considering that concept and each subsequent word, phrase, image,
etc. This is just one way of getting your thoughts out. Your mindmap
can take the form of a list, stream of consciousness, associative writing,
poetry, prose, doodling, or something else entirely.

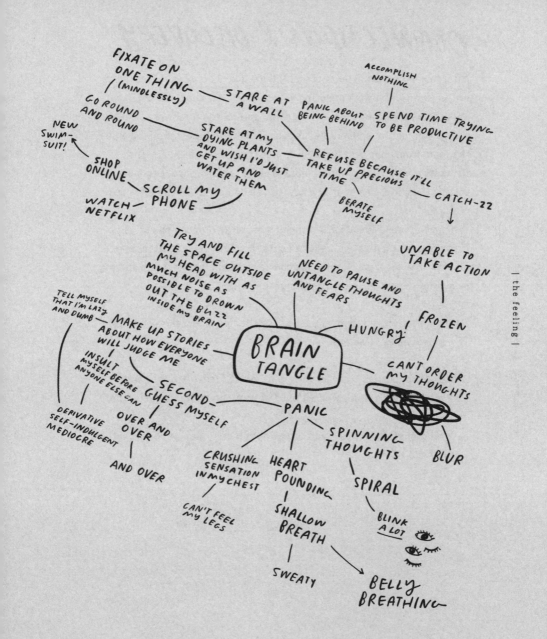

FIXATE ON ONE THING (MINDLESSLY)

STARE AT A WALL

PANIC ABOUT BEING BEHIND

ACCOMPLISH NOTHING

SPEND TIME TRYING TO BE PRODUCTIVE

GO ROUND AND ROUND

NEW SWIM-SUIT!

SHOP ONLINE

STARE AT MY DYING PLANTS AND WISH I'D JUST GET UP AND WATER THEM

REFUSE BECAUSE IT'LL TAKE UP PRECIOUS TIME

CATCH-22

SCROLL MY PHONE

WATCH NETFLIX

BERATE MYSELF

UNABLE TO TAKE ACTION

TRY AND FILL THE SPACE OUTSIDE MY HEAD WITH AS MUCH NOISE AS POSSIBLE TO DROWN OUT THE BUZZ INSIDE MY BRAIN

NEED TO PAUSE AND UNTANGLE THOUGHTS AND FEARS

FROZEN

TELL MYSELF THAT I'M LAZY AND DUMB

MAKE UP STORIES ABOUT HOW EVERYONE WILL JUDGE ME

HUNGRY!

INSULT MYSELF BEFORE ANYONE ELSE CAN

SECOND-GUESS MYSELF

BRAIN TANGLE

CAN'T ORDER MY THOUGHTS

DERIVATIVE SELF-INDULGENT MEDIOCRE

OVER AND OVER

PANIC

SPINNING THOUGHTS

BLUR

AND OVER

CRUSHING SENSATION IN MY CHEST

HEART POUNDING

SPIRAL

CAN'T FEEL MY LEGS

SHALLOW BREATH

BLINK A LOT

SWEATY

BELLY BREATHING

CONNECTIONS & DISCOVERY

After releasing the contents of your mind, take a step back. This is the tender and careful work of seeing yourself without shame or judgment. Make some breathing room between you and all the fragmented, messy things you just let spill onto your page. This might mean walking across the room from your paper and viewing it at some physical distance. Drinking a full glass of water before reading back through. Or maybe setting it aside for an hour or a day, so you can return with fresh eyes.

When you're ready, read back through your mind dump with curiosity. If you feel yourself assigning judgments to what you've written, take a breath. Then let it go. Nothing is good or bad here. Let your pen and paper be a morally neutral space. Anything is possible.

1. Find a pattern; are there any repeating themes or words or phrases? Which feel most pressing?

2. Look for opposites; are there any conflicting ideas? Are they *both* true? Can you imagine a world where they aren't in opposition to each other?

3. What's missing? As you read back through your map, is there anything you want to add?

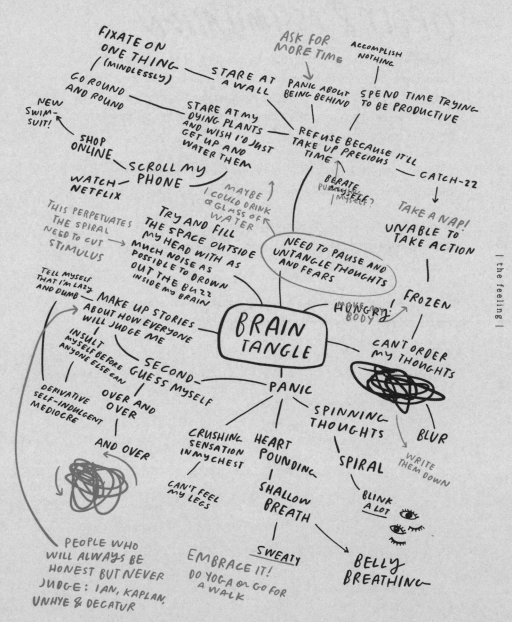

FIXATE ON ONE THING (MINDLESSLY)

GO ROUND AND ROUND

NEW SWIM-SUIT!

SHOP ONLINE

SCROLL MY PHONE

WATCH NETFLIX

ASK FOR MORE TIME

ACCOMPLISH NOTHING

STARE AT A WALL

PANIC ABOUT BEING BEHIND

SPEND TIME TRYING TO BE PRODUCTIVE

STARE AT MY DYING PLANTS AND WISH I'D JUST GET UP AND WATER THEM

REFUSE BECAUSE IT'LL TAKE UP PRECIOUS TIME

CATCH-22

MAYBE I COULD DRINK A GLASS OF WATER

BERATE PUNISH MYSELF?

TAKE A NAP!

UNABLE TO TAKE ACTION

THIS PERPETUATES THE SPIRAL NEED TO CUT STIMULUS

TRY AND FILL THE SPACE OUTSIDE MY HEAD WITH AS MUCH NOISE AS POSSIBLE TO DROWN OUT THE BUZZ INSIDE MY BRAIN

NEED TO PAUSE AND UNTANGLE THOUGHTS AND FEARS

MOVE MY BODY?

HUNGRY!

FROZEN

TELL MYSELF THAT I'M LAZY AND DUMB

MAKE UP STORIES ABOUT HOW EVERYONE WILL JUDGE ME

INSULT MYSELF BEFORE ANYONE ELSE CAN

SECOND-GUESS MYSELF

OVER AND OVER

DERIVATIVE SELF-INDULGENT MEDIOCRE

AND OVER

BRAIN TANGLE

PANIC

CAN'T ORDER MY THOUGHTS

SPINNING THOUGHTS

BLUR

WRITE THEM DOWN

CRUSHING SENSATION IN MY CHEST

HEART POUNDING

SPIRAL

CAN'T FEEL MY LEGS

SHALLOW BREATH

BLINK A LOT

SWEATY

BELLY BREATHING

PEOPLE WHO WILL ALWAYS BE HONEST BUT NEVER JUDGE: IAN, KAPLAN, UNHYE & DECATUR

EMBRACE IT! DO YOGA OR GO FOR A WALK

ORDER & ASSIMILATION

Here we want to make an action plan to integrate what you've discovered through your bodymap into your art/life/beliefs/body. This step is about taking action, whether that be a shift in understanding or planning a new project. Narrow in on one or two things. You don't have to tackle every feeling at once.

1. What do you understand about the central idea you were mapping that you didn't before? How will you it inform your art, beliefs, life, and body?

2. What do you want or need? Is there something that needs to be communicated? Through what lens or point of view do you want to work within? What is your filter?

3. Do you want to channel this energy? Shift it into something else? Or simply sit with it? Do you want to make something just for you? Or will you share it with others?

THINGS TO DO WHEN MY BRAIN IS IN A TANGLE

① REDUCE NOISE
(STOP SCROLLING, SHOPPING OR BINGING THINGS)

② DRINK WATER

③ MOVE BODY

④ WRITE IT DOWN
- ALL MY FEARS
- THINGS I NEED TO DO
(action items, step by step)

I NEED A PLAN, ACTIONABLE STEPS TO TAKE SO I DON'T HAVE TO THINK

THE MOMENT I NOTICE I'M IN A SPIRAL I NEED TO IMMEDIATELY START WRITING SO I DON'T GET CAUGHT IN SELF-LOATHING, AND MOVE MY BODY TO KEEP OUT OF THE GREAT FREEZE
(change positions, stretch, go for a walk)

☐ STOP THE SCROLL

☐ BREATHE DEEPLY UNTIL YOU FEEL SOFTER

☐ MOVE BODY UNTIL YOU FEEL WARM

☐ DRINK WATER (AND MAYBE HAVE A BIT OF SUGAR☺)

NOTE FEARS

WHAT ARE YOU AVOIDING

63

WHAT HAPPENS NEXT??

Sometimes all you need is
to acknowledge your thoughts,
feelings, sensations, etc., and give
them a place to rest on the page,
in which case, hooray! Carry on
with your day.

But often, those practices invite
deeper investigation. That's what
this next section of the book is all
about, so what do you want to do
with what you've discovered?

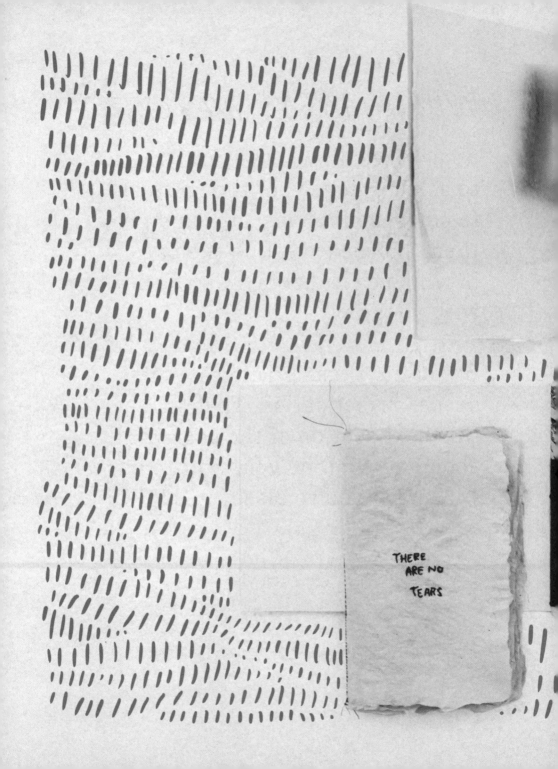

THERE
ARE NO
TEARS

PART TWO
THE MAKING

SHOP BUY THINGS
123 PLACE DR.

THIS THING   4.25
THAT THING   5.00
MORE THINGS   7.25

TOTAL   16.50
CASH   20.00
CHANGE   3.50

RECEIPT

a ROCK

↳ STICKY NOTES

MARK-MAKING TOOLS

STICKS

YOUR PHONE CAMERA →

SLO-MO VIDEO PHOTO PORTRAIT PANO

SCISSORS →

GLUE

a LEAF →

NAPKIN

THE NEWSPAPER

↳ NEWSPAPER or MAGAZINE

You don't need me to tell you how to express yourself or document your days; how to let the full weight of what it means to be human flow through your fingers and onto a page. We have been creating tangible representations of our experiences to make sense of the world for thousands of years. If you're suddenly feeling the urge to carry on about whether or not you're any good at "art," if you have the time for it, or all the necessary supplies, then hear me loud and clear: You already have everything you need. If you don't think you're good at "art-making," call it "mark-making." Anyone can make marks. No caveats, no excuses. Use your three-year-old's broken crayons, swipe that half-dried-up Sharpie, fold down a receipt, scribble something on that napkin (the greasy one you just wiped your pizza fingers on). I honestly do not care how or with what, just that you do. *LOVE YA MEAN IT*

When I say you have everything you need to make things, I mean it. And it's also really nice to have someone offer a framework for practices you haven't tried before. The rest of these pages hold prompts, guides, and tutorials for writing, drawing, and other forms of creating. Please view them as the gentlest offerings from me to you.

What you create in collaboration with the thoughts, ideas, and feelings you uncover will depend on how much time you have, what tools and materials are available to you, your capacity or physical energy, and whether you want to sustain, channel, or shift your emotions.

How do you want to be in relationship with the thoughts, ideas, and feelings swirling around inside you? Do you want to sustain your grief, make ceremony around it, allow it to wash over you? Do you want to find an outlet for your rage? Perhaps you could channel it into a social justice movement close to your heart. Would you like to shift your fears into your gratitude? What practices might help you deepen a sense of awe?

Are you struggling to get out of bed each day? Or are you bounding with pent-up energy? What do you need to find a steady place within yourself? Do you need something to pull you up? Or a place to ground down?

We all operate at different levels of intensity. Establishing your baseline helps you know when you're moving away from your grounded self. I find art-making to be the most useful way to bring myself up out of the dark depths—or down from a disconnected buzz.

ANXIOUS - FRENETIC - MANIC - BUZZING -

MY VISION IS BLURRY, I CAN'T
FOCUS OR PROCESS INFORMATION,
I'M HYPERVIGILANT, CAN'T FEEL
MY BODY, EASILY AGITATED,
BREATH IS SHALLOW & FAST

I CAN FEEL MY LEGS, I AM EASILY
PATIENT WITH MY TINY HUMAN,
I CAN SIT QUIETLY WITHOUT DISCOMFORT

BASE
LINE -

MY BREATH IS STEADY, I CAN
FOLLOW A THOUGHT WITHOUT
OVERWHELM, I PAUSE FOR
TINY DELIGHTS

MY ARMS FEEL HEAVY, I WANT TO
GO TO SLEEP, I'M DISCONNECTED
FROM MY SURROUNDINGS,
ZONING OUT & AVOIDANT AF

DEPRESSED - MELANCHOLIC - EXAUSTED - FROZEN

WANT TO GET NERDY? LOOK INTO THE WINDOW of
TOLERANCE, DEVELOPED BY DAN SIEGEL.

In order to remain in a steady place within yourself, do you need to sustain, channel, or shift your feeling through art-making?

SUSTAIN
Remain in your current state by observing and taking note of the sensations present for you. Try documenting your immediate context, create a ritual to honor how you're feeling.

CHANNEL
Take what you're feeling and use it as momentum or fodder, put it into your work. Can you make something expressive or disruptive with the energy your feelings are generating?

SHIFT
Transform the feeling by engaging in a conversation between the various parts of yourself and the sensations within your body. Or release the feeling by making something expressive.

OKAY! LET'S BREAK EACH OF THESE DOWN →

RITUAL

CEREMONY, INTEGRATION, INTIMACY, HONOR, PRESENCE, STILLNESS

Ritual can be an intricate series of practices, but more often than not it takes the shape of tiny moments in the eye of a toddler tornado.

Pre-pandemic/parenthood, I luxuriated in early morning stillness, waking before the sun, fully rested by 5 AM; candles, incense, morning pages, tarot, tea, and yoga. It was as delightful as it sounds and it is completely unsustainable for me now (and probably most of you too). These days my morning ritual consists of a two-minute scribble that grounds me into my body and a few written words detailing something I've noticed. This is often done with a toddler attached to my legs or wriggling about on my lap. I've turned my morning practice into something much simpler than it used to be: After swallowing my daily meds, I do a blind contour portrait of myself and jot down the first thing that comes to mind as the title.

Rituals don't need to be difficult or complex to matter. This daily nibble at my art practice quickly morphs into a sketchbook filled with self-portraits. This practice offers me a moment of pause each morning as well as an artifact to mark these blurry days where I wake to my face being patted by tiny hands attached to a squirmy body doing acrobatics across the bed. I don't spring from my pillow anymore, I stay nestled in, savoring the alternating sweet pats and wild whacks of my wee one's springy limbs until the numbers on the clock elicit more anxiety than the bed holds comfort. But no matter how late we might be, I can always spare two minutes. Two minutes of presence with my reflection in the mirror and an acknowledgment of at least one thought in my head.

I set myself up for success with this ritual by gathering my tools and giving them a home in the spot I'll use them. Most importantly, I didn't just fling a ritual into my day all willy-nilly; I gave it a piggyback ride on a pre-existing habit. I always take my medicine in the morning, so I bought a pill case with a mirror and put it in a jar on my kitchen table along with a pen and a tiny sketchbook for my daily drawings.

Rituals can also be born by accident. For example: I captured the commute from my house to my studio in a fifteen-second video on the first day I crept out for a full day of work in my very own space. All I included in the frame were my feet walking across the toy-strewn muddy yard to my garage-turned-studio. I recorded it in a rush of excitement, not intending to repeat it or thinking any more about it than that it would make a cute story on my Instagram. But that thrill has yet to fade. Every time I make my way to the doors of my studio it feels like the first. I hope the prickle of gratitude never stops spreading goosebumps across my skin, and I continue this practice of recording the steps between my safe dwelling and this room of my own. Such abundance calls for acknowledgment; this simple practice does just that.

WHAT DO YOU NEED?
CAN YOU GIVE YOURSELF THAT THING THROUGH ART-MAKING?

LET THE ACT of CREATING BE WHAT NOURISHES YOU.

WHATEVER RESULTS IS SIMPLY AN ARTIFACT OF TIME SPENT CARING FOR YOURSELF.

YOUR TURN!

Can you litter your days with moments of ritual that connect you to a sense of grandeur while inviting stillness within yourself?

Consider transitions: just before this or right after that. See where you already have a habit and piggyback on it with a ritual.

Set yourself up for success. Make your rituals small, achievable, nourishing, and delightful. They should give more than they take from you. Prepare yourself for them. Set the stage. Be realistic about your time and energy.

Take note of patterns. Do you always feel drawn to take a picture of the same tree? Could you make it a regular practice that you attend to with intention?

Notice what delights you, but also be aware of what is missing. Can you fill an empty spot in your schedule, heart, or home with a nourishing practice?

WANNA DIG DEEPER?

For Small Creatures Such as We: Rituals for Finding Meaning in Our Unlikely World by Sasha Sagan

The Power of Moment: Why Certain Experiences Have Extraordinary Impact by Chip Heath and Dan Heath

"Rules of Engagement" TEDx Talk by Kate Bingaman Burt

KATE BINGAMAN-BURT

YOU TEACH US ABOUT REGULARITY
AND REPETITION AS YOU DOCUMENT THE
WAY WE LIVE AND WHAT WE CONSUME.
I'VE LEARNED HOW TO CRAFT A PRACTICE OF
RITUAL FOR MYSELF BY WITNESSING
YOUR PROCESS. THANK YOU ♡

OCT 16. 2021

my hair
is out of
control

← my head
aches
but i like in
my neck

SAD
Tummy

Need to get
thick socks
↓

forget how
long it takes
← to break in
Docs.
OUCH!

BOUGHT NEW
BOOTS SO NOW
I'M READY TO
SMASH THE
PATRIARCHY

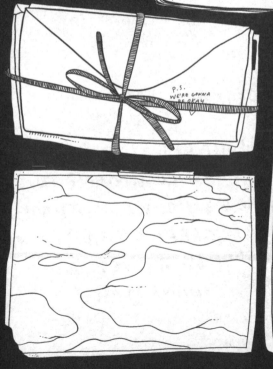

P.S.
WE'RE GONNA
BE OKAY
↓

8:00

Instagram

CAITIE_METZ

♡ Q ◁

Breathe ♥

CAITIE_METZ Drink a glass of water.
Charge your vibrator. Take your meds.
I love you.

Add a comment...

CAITIE_METZ

DOCUMENTATION

TRACKING, REMEMBERING, OBSERVATION, ORDER, CHRONICLE, PROOF

Documentation can be a lot of things, from list making to poetry, intricate drawings of everything you eat or portraits taken at regular intervals to mark growth. For me, it is integrated into every part of my tiny existence, in my medium-sized town, in this great big world. This method of art-making permeates all of the various ways I create; it can be a ritual or expression, a conversation and form of disruption. There's a line in one of my favorite songs by Cloud Cult that says, "If ever I can't see the magic around me, please take my hands off my eyes." It's a phrase I have written over and over for myself as a reminder to be awake to the life happening all around me. I don't ever want to catch myself thinking "if only I'd enjoyed that time." I want to know how deeply precious and wondrous these boring, silly, tedious, beautiful moments are as they happen. I want to memorialize my life while I'm alive. I do this by documenting every little thing through photographs, drawings, and writing.

Recording your life is a way of creating a field guide for yourself. Every time you note a feeling, sensation, or idea, it's like dropping a pin on the map of your life. These markers serve as memorials and directives. You can look back and know you have indeed made it through a hard thing before and will again. You can document like an archivist, collecting moments and memories to keep you warm on cold nights, or as a scientist, plotting data to cross reference your past and present experiences.

I am a cartographer, storyteller, and analyst.

I scribble drawings of the clothes that give me a sense of gender euphoria so I might later have a record of what feels good on my body. I fill my camera roll with videos of me and my tiny bean, often in a blur of tickles and kisses—tiny portals we can travel back to anytime we wish. I document the sky out of wistful admiration but also as a tether to mark this time and place. Here I am, a tiny speck of the cosmos, and this is what the sky looks like just as I witness Brandi Carlile for the first time in concert, as the walls to my new studio are put in place, and as I submit the manuscript for this book. These photos feel more like self-portraits than landscapes of the clouds; in them I am transcendent and gloriously insignificant. I leave all the things I make in this life as a trail of crumbs or flickering lights, something to reference when I look back, or guide the way forward. I deeply believe the wider the range of human experience documented, the more we will belong together in a weird and delightful state of nonjudgement. Brené Brown talks about normalizing things for her kids so they don't experience shame (particularly around bodies), and I think that's what documentational work has done for me. Seeing a wide range of stories, experiences, ideas, and identities, each different than my own, ease my fear about not lining up with one perfect way of being. At the other end of the spectrum, it feels like a homecoming to witness my experience being named by someone else. I immediately feel like weeping when I come across images or words that mirror back to me what I've been experiencing. I hope the things I choose to archive and record do the same for others. This is how we make the world a little less lonely. This is how we say my story is true and so is yours. And the tension between multiple realities is what gives form and dimension to our world.

IN THE WORDS
OF MARY OLIVER,
"PAY ATTENTION,
BE ASTONISHED,
TELL ABOUT IT."

YOUR TURN!

Grab your phone or favorite camera and wander around your house. Take photos as a neutral observer. Let every pile, overflowing closet, and tuft of dog hair be a still life waiting to be framed. Can you find any gallery-worthy installations or performance pieces created by those who inhabit your home? What beauty can you find among the mayhem?

Collect and archive anything you're drawn to: save scraps of paper, tickets, notes, paint chips, and create a visual or written archive of your favorite items.

Give yourself a tiny daily project that records just a sliver of your life. Choose something you're curious about or want to preserve. Document it through a photo, drawing, words, or audio, etc. It must be doable within three to five minutes and with materials that are easily accessible to you (consider how you might ritualize this practice for your daily life, see pg. 74).

WANNA DIG DEEPER?

Anything written by Mary Oliver
Dear Data by Giorgia Lupi and Stefanie Posavec
Kate Bingaman-Burt's daily purchase drawings
Moorea Seal's 52 Lists series

MARY OLIVER

EVERY TIME I READ YOUR POEMS
I GET THE INEXPLICABLE URGE TO
GO DOCUMENT THE WORLD THROUGH
MY OWN EYES SO I MIGHT BE ABLE
TO SINK DEEPLY INTO THIS ONE
WILD AND PRECIOUS LIFE.
I LOVE YOU FOREVER, YOU
SHOWED ME THE WAY.

CONVERSATION

CONTEXT, CONNECTION, ZEITGEIST, ASSOCIATION, EXCHANGE, DISCOURSE

You can make work in conversation with many things, but since this is a book about making things with your feels, I'm going to focus on being in conversation with yourself.

It's 2016, I'm in my early twenties, figuring out what it means to be queer, married, and a graduate student. I've yet to start therapy and I'm wavering between familial responsibilities and forging my own path. I'm trying to disentangle gender from sexuality and find common ground between my need for freedom and stability. And so I'm clinging to the notion that there could be many truths and desires within my body at once. Perhaps if they could talk to one another, I wouldn't feel so torn apart. What if the contradictions weren't actually incongruent? So I began painting messages, accusations, warnings, invitations, and fears across my skin with slick, acrylic paint. I took a series of self-portraits, blew up those images, and papered my walls with them, a backdrop for another round of photographs. This series was an intricate conversation with myself. Both an investigation of who I was and an invitation to continue becoming.

Years later when I finally started therapy (bless!) I was introduced to IFS (also known as "parts work") and holy shit, it was like someone switched on a light bulb. Not metaphorically, but like really, really truly. I could see and understand parts of myself that I'd been groping around in the dark for my whole life. I felt such a deep relief. *Everything I felt was valid and real, but it didn't make it true*. There were vast stories and beliefs inside and now I had the tools to distinguish myself from my inner child, from wounded parts, and protectors, etc. I just had to listen with compassion and care.

As I've been writing this book, I have woven myself into countless sticky tangles. It's a white hot blur that leaves me paralyzed for weeks on end, missing deadlines and avoiding emails from my editor (sorry, Sara). When I finally stop and ask all the shadows to write down their worries, I learn that one is terrified of what others will think of me as a designer (kerning, negative space, pacing, layout, typeface, etc.); another has a looming fear about what my parents will think of me when they read this. And what about my mentors and past professors, peers and my students? Am I parading as an expert on things which I've only just scratched the surface?

In deep conflict with these fears is an uncompromising insistence on being honest and real about my experience, and a timid belief that might soften some corner of the world just a little bit. As you can see, it's a wild kerfuffle. But when I validate the fears swirling within, letting them know I'm not a little kid getting bullied for being bad at spelling anymore, that I don't have to assimilate or to perform to perfection to belong to my community, they settle down, watching wide-eyed as I surge forward, their wails of terror now quiet. I can calm my inner selves with gentle reminders that we are all safe. I am the grown-up in charge here.

Making conversational work allows me to breathe space in between stimulus and response, come to a deeper understanding of myself, and untangle conflicting values, beliefs, fears, and desires. Conversing with the swirling thoughts in my head illuminates the murky spaces, where feelings cast shadows three times their size. When I'm able to untangle my mind onto the page, I find that the big scaries usually shrink into something resembling a scared or lonely child.

It's as simple as letting your thoughts all spill out on the page, helter-skelter, nonsensical, and irreverent. I communicate best in fragments, words drawn together by lines and images (thus my love of mapping my body and mind) as my thoughts come like popcorn constellations, erupting suddenly with little pops, sprinkled about like stars. Once I orient myself, I'm able to trace lines between various thoughts or worries to create a shape that leads the way toward understanding and self-compassion.

IS THERE ANYTHING MORE VALIDATING THAN BEING INVITED INTO A CONVERSATION WITHOUT JUDGMENT OR ASSUMPTIONS, JUST OPEN CURIOSITY? NOW IMAGINE TURNING THAT TYPE OF CARE INWARD. WHAT A FUCKING GIFT.

YOUR TURN!

Next time you feel conflicted or overwhelmed, try making a mindmap (see page 54).

(see page 54).

1. Begin by writing down the thing you are overwhelmed by in the center of your page.

2. Allow your thoughts to tumble out onto the paper in a web around your central worry.

3. Once you've emptied yourself, see if you can find common themes and group them together.

4. Can you validate each point of view? Could you write out a conversation between them to see what each of the perspectives has to say?

5. What can you learn from all of these?

6. What exists in between them?

7. Where does this constellation of fear, belief, desire, etc., lead you?

This process unmuddles that sticky spaghetti mess like nobody's business. It's like wiping the fog off your bathroom mirror or finally getting the right prescription glasses. Everything comes into focus, and even if you still don't know the solution, you know what you're working with. And that's half the battle.

Speak gently to yourself; you're building the voice that will narrate your future, and all your younger selves are listening.

WANNA DIG DEEPER?

Your Illustrated Guide to Becoming One With the Universe by Yumi Sakugawa
No Bad Parts: Healing Trauma and Restoring Wholeness with the Internal Family Systems Model by Richard C. Schwartz

YUMI SAKUGAWA

YOUR WORDS AND DRAWINGS OPENED A CHANNEL THROUGH WHICH I CAN BE IN CONVERSATION WITH MYSELF AND THE UNIVERSE. YOU'RE A RARE GIFT. YOU'VE SHOWN ME HOW VAST AND BEAUTIFUL THE WORLD INSIDE OF ME CAN BE.

UNLIMITED PERMISSION GRANTED to feel it all · ADMIT EVERYONE

REMAIN SENSITIVE NOW & ALWAYS

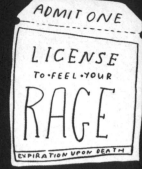
ADMIT ONE
LICENSE TO·FEEL·YOUR RAGE
EXPIRATION UPON DEATH

IT'S OKAY to NOT FEEL OOKAY

THROUGH EXPRESS YOURSELF VISUALS · LIFETIME

DAILY STAY TENDER DAILY

INTERNAL EXPLORATION UNLIMITED ACCESS

N. 9559308 AUTHORIZATION TO BE PETTY AF

SHOUT OUT ABOUT JOY · WHENEVER YOU CAN

N°1365278
LET IT OUT

VIP PASS
PERMISSION TO ★ FEEL IT ALL ★
— VALID FOR ENTIRE LIFE —

MELT DOWN ONE · MELT DOWN ONE · MELT DOWN ONE · MELT DOWN ONE

EXPRESSION

RELEASE, CLARITY, PROCLAMATION, VOICING, SHARING, LIBERATION

Expressive mark-making is like opening the release valve on your emotional instapot and letting the rush of steam release from your body. That's how it feels for me when I take a photo of myself mid-cry or when I write furiously into my notes app (instead of sending an angry text). I use art as an escape route, a pillow to scream into, or a rooftop to shout from, be it in pain, joy, or terror.

The day our forty-fifth president was elected, after a sleepless night of dry-heaving sobs, I went to my studio and gathered letters from my typecase to spell out the phrase "not my president." I set the blocks of lead, locked them into the chaise, and began printing sheet after sheet of paper with these words in bold black ink. It wasn't revolutionary or original (this sentiment was floating all around the internet), but it served as a meditation and physical release. Every time the plates closed on the press bed, imprinting the paper, each time I heard the soft sizzle of my rollers turning across the ink disk I felt the chant *not my president, not my president, not my president* loosening the grief in my body. I sat for hours addressing envelopes to everyone who had DMed me on Instagram asking for one of these cards. Every time I stuffed an envelope, I felt a tiny ping of connection to the recipient. It didn't solve anything, but printing those cards and sending them to strangers around the country got me through that awful day. We weren't alone in this moment.

As I write this, my face is puffy from crying and my hands are shaking from the emotion surging through me. Today, Roe v. Wade was overturned and, in a cruel series of events, it's also the day my beloved local coffee shop closed forever. Maybe it seems silly or dramatic to you who might not know of St. Louis's Rise Coffee House, but it feels like the whole fucking world is ending. I am numb, but also electric. Like I'm made of stone, but also about to implode. Grief pulses in my stomach alongside punches of nausea in step with the beating of my heart. The place I found complete belonging and safety just closed on the same day that my government decided that my body is not my own. It's too much. How am I to hold all this? Where do I put this rage? This grief? It's manifesting as incredible tension in my arms and back and a throbbing head. I know that if I don't tend to these feelings, they'll transmute into bitterness or a breakdown, or both. I must release it—express the depth and range of emotion ricocheting inside my body. And maybe make something that will soften the grief and rage of those around me.

So I'm going to make a zine. Something to commemorate the place I loved most in the world, Rise Coffee House. Something to honor what it means to me and to keep the spirit of that place alive in me. Something for the throngs of people who wound down the street in an endless line since the closing was announced last week. Something that might validate their tears over a coffee shop when they start to feel a little silly for weeping over four walls and a latte. Because it wasn't just anything. It was a movement, a moment, a world we built together. Then I'm going to write a letter to my body, letting it know we're safe. That we're a team, and that we're going to fight like hell for the dignity of safe, accessible, comprehensive healthcare for all.

THIS IS WHAT EXPRESSIVE WORK LOOKS LIKE FOR ME IN THIS MOMENT. WHAT FORM WILL IT TAKE FOR YOU? CAN YOU UNBURDEN YOURSELF THROUGH CREATION? I'LL LEAVE YOU WITH WORDS BY SUSAN CAIN—"WHATEVER PAIN YOU CAN'T GET RID OF, MAKE IT YOUR CREATIVE OFFERING."

JOUR TURN!

What is it you want to make known? What, if left unsaid, will eat away at your insides?

What if the next time you were really angry you snatched up the nearest piece of paper and wrote down all the things you'd like to say or do? Give yourself an immediate release instead of acting out of that anger.

Does grief ever threaten to swallow you whole? Could you give it a space to live on the page?

When did you last gush about the things you love?

FEEL SOMETHING, MAKE SOMETHING. RINSE & REPEAT.

WANNA DIG DEEPER?

Anything ever painted by Frida Kahlo

Bittersweet: How Sorrow and Longing Make Us Whole by Susan Cain

Music or poetry that makes you cry/sing/dance

FRIDA KAHLO

THANK YOU FOR MAKING SUCH
RICH PAINTINGS ABOUT WHAT IT
IS TO BE ALIVE AND FOR TEACHING
US WHAT IT IS TO LOVE AND LOSE
AND GRIEVE OUT LOUD.
YOU'RE FOREVER IN MY HEART.

DISRUPTION

DECONSTRUCTION, SUBVERSION, DOUBT,
CONFRONTATION, QUESTIONING

In his 1962 essay "The Creative Process," James Baldwin calls the artist "the incorrigible disturber of the peace." He goes on to say, "The artist cannot and must not take anything for granted, but must drive to the heart of every answer and expose the questions the answer hides."

Not taking things for granted is quite a childlike way to approach the world. I like to call it "practicing non-assumption." As I watch my tiny one investigate the world, I can't think of anything more apt to call him than an incorrigible disturber of the peace. Nothing is safe from that sweet babe's curious eye. Everything must be tasted, chewed, or checked for audible resonance against multiple surfaces before ultimately being thrown aside. I try and encourage as much of this as possible. Unless there is imminent danger, we tinker, bang, and taste. We do it wrong, backwards, and upside down. Who's to say which way is the right way to use a spoon? Or that tables shouldn't be sat upon? If we all gleefully perched atop raised surfaces, what fresh perspectives would we find? Our innate desire to try to uncover things for ourselves, to understand and make our own meaning, is scolded out of us by the pressure to conform, not make a fuss, and keep the peace. In my humble opinion, adopting feigned courtesy and manners instead of earnest curiosity and desire is a terrible way to live.

Disruptive mark-making doesn't have to be loud or impertinent.

Sometimes the most disruptive thing you can do is pause and examine the origin of your values and beliefs. To ask "Why?" What if you sat quietly with all the things you have accepted without question, that live deep within your body? Can you embody your inner three-year-old and ask *why* upon *why*, followed by yet another *why*? Not out of obstinance but a deep thirst for understanding. Can you honestly say you know why you act, say, think, and believe the things you do? What might you upend if you weren't posturing toward beliefs that you don't actually want to uphold?

Disruption looks like asking myself what I deeply, truly want.

It's a disassembling of all the parts that make up a life and reordering them in the configuration that suits me and the ones I love best. I've engaged with disruption lately by pausing to explore tiny ants scurrying around on the ground, photographing the sky, and asking for what I need. I parent with gentleness, treating my child as a whole human being, even when it might make others uncomfortable or annoyed.

KNOWING WHAT YOU
BELIEVE MAKES YOU
BRAVE, CURIOUS, AND
STURDY ENOUGH IN
YOURSELF TO STAND UP,
SPEAK OUT, AND
ROCK THE BOAT A LITTLE.

YOUR TURN!

Do you uphold rules just to go with the flow? What would happen if you didn't?

Where did your beliefs come from? Are they yours or someone else's? Where are there inconsistencies between your actions and beliefs? When did you last evaluate your motivations or examine your habitual gestures, phrases, and actions? Have you spent any time working to understand the positions, opinions, desires, and needs of those you stand in opposition to?

Uncover your whys by crafting a manifesto (see page 146 for a guide) or a list of guiding principles once a season. This will help you stay nimble, adjusting to what is just in front of you instead of trying to create rigid rules for your whole life.

Every time you encounter a rule, constraint, belief, or value this week, take it as an opportunity to ask why, to peer underneath and behind each one and ask, *Where did you come from? Who/what does this protect/support? Who/what does it harm/limit?*

WANNA DIG DEEPER?

The Crossroads of Should and Must: Find and Follow Your Passion by Elle Luna

Beyond the Gender Binary by Alok Vaid-Menon

The Live Your Values Deck: Sort Out, Honor, and Practice What Matters Most to You by Lisa Congdon and Andreea Niculescu

The Way of Integrity by Martha Beck

ALOK VAID-MENON

YOU HAVE SHOWN ME THAT DISRUPTION
ISN'T ABOUT BRUTE FORCE, RATHER IT
IS THE ART OF PERSISTENTLY BEING ONESELF
WITHOUT SHYING AWAY FROM PRECARIOUS JOY.
A SOFTER, BRAVER LESSON CANNOT BE FOUND.
THANK YOU, THANK YOU.

In summary, here are some clouds to illustrate the intersection of these functions in my life.

And to remind you that none of this happens in a vacuum. It's all intertwined. Let my categorization of these functions of art-making inspire you to investigate your own practices and find the threads that weave their way through your work.

I want to document these days by making a ritual of recurring tasks, honoring these moments that are at once unending and fleeting. This disrupts the rush, the desire to skim over the awkward, to polish up ourselves as though we're not all just soft animal bodies desperately trying to love the thing they love (thanks, Mary Oliver). The slower and more present I am in my practice and everyday life, the more I crack open, expressing all the hungry wonder and raging grief inside me, and the more honest my conversation with the universe becomes.

Making things is the most human thing we can do.
AMEN, AMEN, and AMEN.

① TAKE PHOTOS OF THE SKY EVERY DAY (SAME PLACE, TIME, ETC) MAKE IT A RITUAL

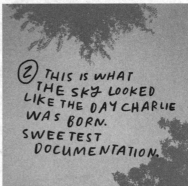

② THIS IS WHAT THE SKY LOOKED LIKE THE DAY CHARLIE WAS BORN. SWEETEST DOCUMENTATION.

③ BE IN RELATIONSHIP WITH THE SKY, LISTEN, HAVE A CONVERSATION

④ SHOUT ABOUT HOW MUCH YOU LOVE THE SKY! EXPRESS!

⑤ FOLLOW THE LONGING, DON'T WORRY ABOUT WHAT OTHERS WILL THINK, DISRUPT WITH JOY.

OKAY, READY
to MAKE SOME
THINGS ⟶

FIRST THINGS FIRST
YOU NEED A CREATIVE STUDIO
SPOILER! IT'S A WAY OF BEING, NOT A PHYSICAL SPACE

Let's make two lists:
1. All the supplies you'd like to have (your dreamiest studio)
2. What you actually need (the very barest essentials)

I'm going to guess that you already have most of the essentials or that they are easily attained. If not, you might want to reevaluate your list of needs and narrow it down. Making things doesn't have to cost you oodles and oodles of time or money. Art-making can be a glorious investment, but you don't have to make a grand gesture to be invited in. In fact, I'd argue that the surest way to the heart of your muse is through a steady and quiet commitment to listening and responding. Fancy materials and expensive tools don't come with a manual for how to notice, process, and feel. You are your most generative and useful resource.

To be clear, I have a well-stocked studio. I'm no minimalist when it comes to art supplies. But the fact is that the everyday, self-expressive, feel-it, make-it work I create usually happens on the fly, at the kitchen table with last week's grocery list and a nearby highlighter. Conditions are rarely perfect. I don't luxuriate in uninterrupted time behind a closed door very often. After all, feelings come when you're in the car, at the park, in the shower, before bed, in waiting rooms, or when you're paying bills. They don't wait until you're perfectly organized with a juicy budget, fresh cup of coffee, and hours of time at your disposal. My aim is to support you in conjuring the conditions necessary to engage in ritual, document, converse, express, and disrupt anytime, anywhere.

If I have pen and paper, I've yet to find a place that can't become my studio.

I can fold, draw, write, trace, scribble, tear, construct, and crumple. So I always have notebooks and favorite pens at the ready (Pilot Precise V7 bought in bulk). I tuck them into the center console of my car, frequently used tote bags, kitchen drawers, on my nightstand, and in the fruit bowl on my dining room table. There is a tiny sketchbook that resides in my fanny pack, a larger one in my backpack, and a sweat-stained Moleskine with my yoga things. I'm strategic about always having my basic tools within arm's reach.

Building a studio for yourself is as much a mindset as it is a collection of the right conditions, lighting, and materials. It's one part having access to the essentials, and one part using whatever the heck is lying around. Making a studio wherever you are means both placing the tools in your path to create and removing obstacles from your mind. These are some of my favorite resources for getting in the right head space.

The Artist's Way by Julia Cameron; *Big Magic* by Elizabeth Gilbert; *Your Illustrated Guide to Becoming One with the Universe* by Yumi Sakugawa; *The Creative Habit* by Twyla Tharp

One of my favorite makers is Adam J. Kurtz, who fashions heartfelt and wondrous artifacts with the simplest materials and in the smallest of spaces. You don't have to be anything more than who you are right now, you don't need anything besides what's right around you. Draw with a stick in the dirt and take a photo of it. Bam, you just created something.

You know who else created the most magnificent, expressive, and important things out of whatever was lying nearby? Basquiat. His work always stops me in my tracks. I got to see a collection of his early work a few years ago, stunning guttural gestures on everything from torn paper and cardboard to milk cartons and discarded metal cans. My god, it was so magnificent.

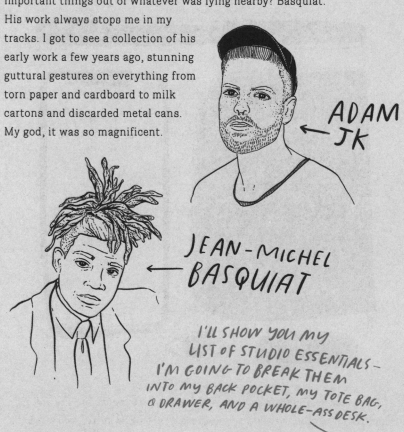

ADAM
JK

JEAN-MICHEL
BASQUIAT

I'LL SHOW YOU MY
LIST OF STUDIO ESSENTIALS—
I'M GOING TO BREAK THEM
INTO MY BACK POCKET, MY TOTE BAG,
A DRAWER, AND A WHOLE-ASS DESK.

THINGS I CARRY IN MY BACK POCKET

Pen, tiny notebook, key chain pocketknife (with tiny scissors!), my phone,* and a keen eye for materials I can use on the fly.

You can take/edit photos and videos, jot down notes, watch YouTube video tutorials, read about a topic you're interested in, look up quotes, connect with creators on social media, etc.

WHAT'S IN MY BACKPACK?!

Journal, sketchbook, pens and other writing apparatuses, sticky notes, iPad and charger, snacks,* water bottle, and at least three books that I'm in various stages of reading.

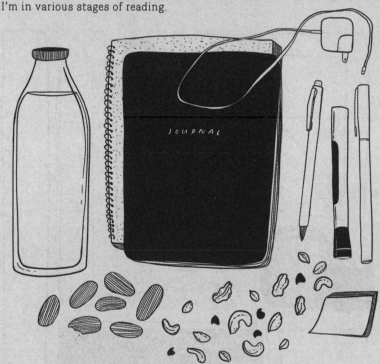

I'm a firm believer that a well-fed and hydrated body makes the best things. Remember: your body is a book, a canvas; it contains memory, knowledge, intuition, your lineage, and so on. You are your dearest resource and your most precious tool. In short, you're a fucking work of art by simply being alive. Tend to yourself well.

THINGS I KEEP IN A DRAWER OF MY OWN

Rulers, envelopes, stamps, sticky notes, scissors, X-Acto blade, glue stick, bone folder, tape, and more snacks (of course).

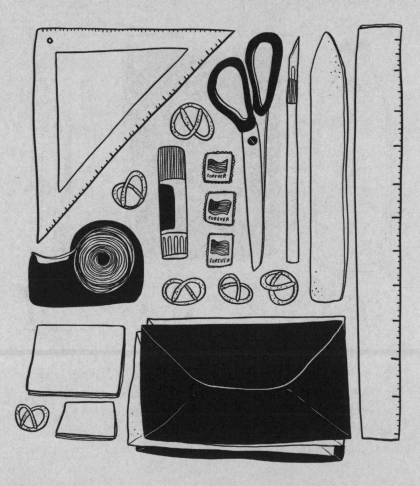

HOW DO I FILL AN ENTIRE DESK?!

Candle, incense, pictures, plants, scanner, printer, light box, hourglass, Sharpies, love notes to myself, and, if possible, a nearby shelf with my collection of books and tarot cards.

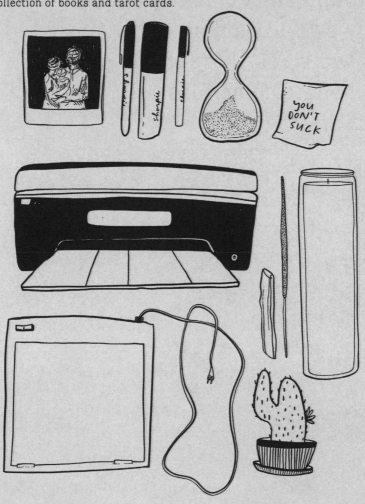

TUTORIALS

These practices/forms have been around since forever, but I do have my own little flair, and I'm excited to walk you through my process. I'll share some tutorials, tips, and prompts.

THIS IS ONE OF MY FAVES
CHEERIO BOX LID
A LOT OF FOLKS HAVE A COPY OF THIS
I DIDN'T THINK ABOUT YOU TODAY.
DATE YOUR SELF
I HAVE A LOT OF CRUSHES
THINGS TO DO WHEN YOU'RE ANXIOUS

ZINES

A zine is a most magical thing: It's a tiny
publication, usually handmade, about a
specific topic. A zine is just a little book or
magazine, or pamphlet. Anyone can make one
about anything. I love zines because they feel
like the perfect container to hold my biggest
and messiest feels.

AIRLINE
TICKET and
STRING

Tools

1. Foldable material
an envelope, notebook paper,
receipt, copy paper, a large leaf, etc.

2. Mark-making tool
a broken crayon, nail polish,
pencil, Sharpie, etc.

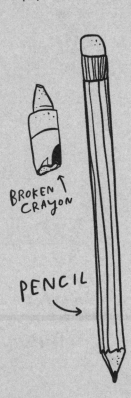

BROKEN
CRAYON

PENCIL

RECEIPT

SOME STORE
OF ALL THE THINGS

THING 1 .... 2.25
THING 2 .... 3.57
THING 3 .... 10.90

ALL THE THINGS 16.72

TOOMUCHSTUFF.COM

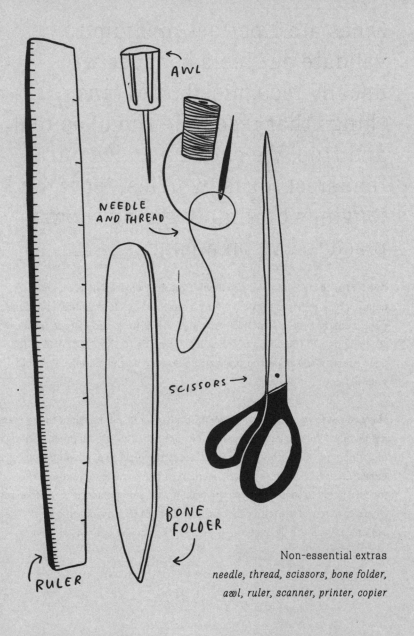

AWL

NEEDLE
AND THREAD

SCISSORS →

BONE
FOLDER

RULER

Non-essential extras
needle, thread, scissors, bone folder,
awl, ruler, scanner, printer, copier

Zines are a perfect medium to validate our feels because we usually recognize books (and things that resemble them) as real and true. We can legitimize our tenderest ideas, worries, fears, and longings by simply giving them a place to live on a page.

I've folded these kinds of zines down from more materials than I can count: a receipt paper torn out of my sketchbook, a sticky note, magazine page, napkin, flyer at the DMV, envelope, 3 × 5-inch card, scraps from the recycling bin . . . the magic of the zines I'm going to share with you is that they adapt to any scale and proportion. So long as the material will fold and tear down, it'll work!

Have you ever wanted to write a book? Do it now. Make the damn thing; there are no rules. Want to create a magazine about the fantastical inner workings of your home? A monthly publication about the process of growing your bangs? Do it! Make a zine about a memory, a place you love, your favorite foods, a guide to something you are brilliant at, your values, or a photo essay. Share an idea you're excited about, a love note to friends, or tell a story. The options are endless. So grab the nearest scrap and get started.

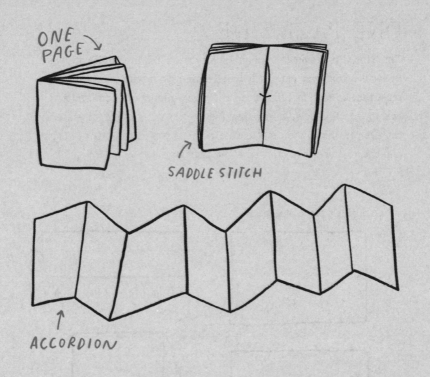

ONE
PAGE

SADDLE STITCH

ACCORDION

THE IDEA OF YOU TURNING
THIS PAGE AND MAKING A ZINE
HAS ME CLAPPING MY HANDS
AND SQUEALING LIKE MY
GLEEFUL TODDLER

ONE-PAGE ZINE

This zine is my favorite (and only) party trick. I'm incredibly awkward in social situations, especially when hanging out with strangers. So trust that as soon as I find a segue, I'll be pulling paper out and getting everyone to fold down a tiny zine. I've been making these for years and they've yet to lose their magic. One moment you have a piece of paper, and the next you're holding an eight-page zine.

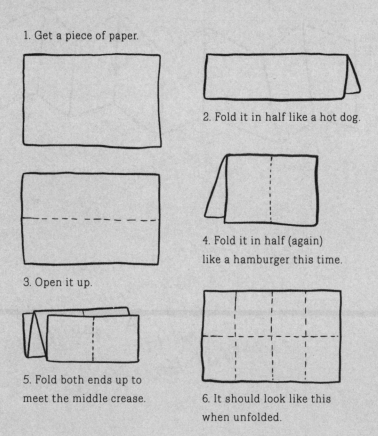

1. Get a piece of paper.

2. Fold it in half like a hot dog.

3. Open it up.

4. Fold it in half (again) like a hamburger this time.

5. Fold both ends up to meet the middle crease.

6. It should look like this when unfolded.

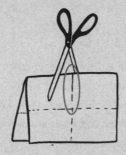
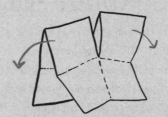

7. Fold your paper back to a hamburger, and cut like so.

8. Using both hands, pinch each side down and out to create...

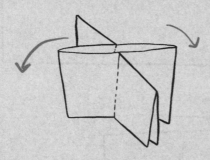

9. A shape like this, then fold it around and in half to make...

10. Your very own zine!!!!

ACCORDIAN-FOLD ZINE

Remember when you were a kid and you'd fold a piece of paper down into a fan? But you'd always have the bit at the end that was just a little too long or short? Perfectionists rejoice, I have the perfect way to fold any piece of paper into evenly spaced sections so you never get an awkward tail again. The trick is to fold both sides at the same time.

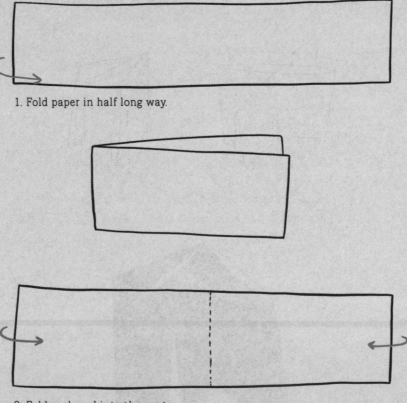

1. Fold paper in half long way.

2. Fold each end into the center.

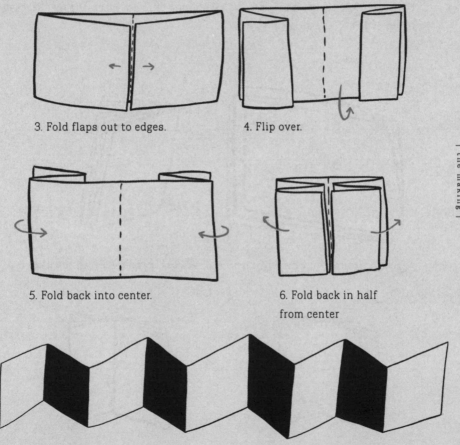

3. Fold flaps out to edges.

4. Flip over.

5. Fold back into center.

6. Fold back in half from center

B-STITCH ZINE

A shockingly simple binding that looks so polished and fresh. I love using this needle-and-thread binding for a little extra pizazz. Try it with thread, ribbon, yarn, or string. You can also ignore the stitching part and just use a rubber band around the stack—just cut, tear, or punch little notches at the top and bottom of the center fold to hold the band. Try combining different sizes of paper stacked together. Let it be playful!

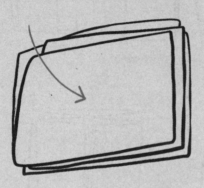

1. Gather a stack of pages (any size).

2. Fold them in half, all together.

3. Open them up.

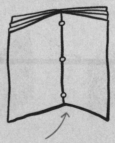

4. Poke three holes along the fold.

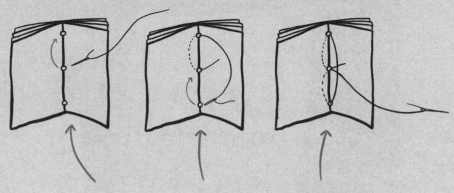

5. Starting with the center hole, push your needle and thread through (make sure to leave a generous tail).

6. Pull your needle back through the top hole, then push through to the back through the bottom hole.

7. Finish by pulling your needle and thread back through the center hole and tying off the tail.

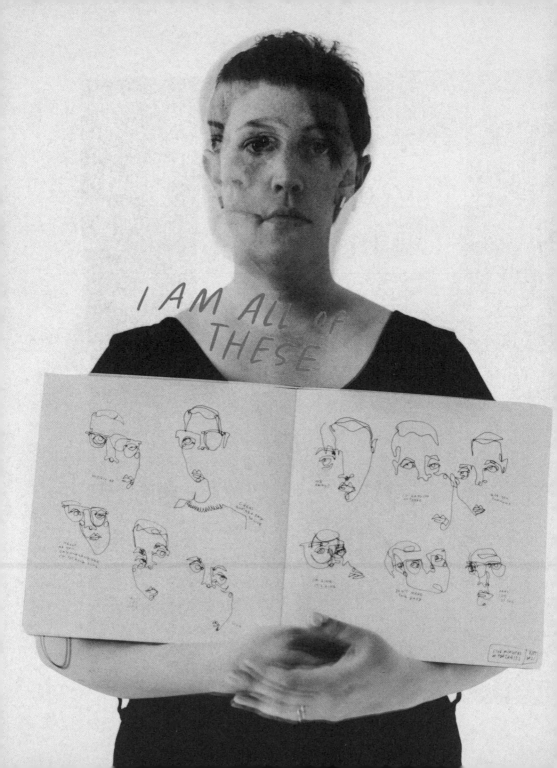

BLIND CONTOUR LINE DRAWING

My dearest practice and steadiest friend. I first learned this style of
drawing my freshman year of college. I hated it because I had so little
control. Now I love them for that very same reason. The honesty and
truth of these lines; my absolutely perfect inability to lie. Drawing
precisely what I see, without looking. This is the sacred work.

OF ALL THE PRACTICES, PROCESSES, AND
MEDIUMS I'VE EXPLORED OVER THE YEARS,
THIS ONE HAS BEEN THE MOST
TRANSFORMATIVE. THESE DRAWINGS
ARE THE MOST INTIMATE RITUAL
AND HAVE CHANGED MY LIFE.

Tools

1. Mark-making tool
pen, pencil, marker, etc.

2. Surface to write on
notebook, scrap of cardboard,
3 × 5-inch card, sticky note,
canvas, etc.

3. Reflective surface
mirror, front-facing camera,
or another person

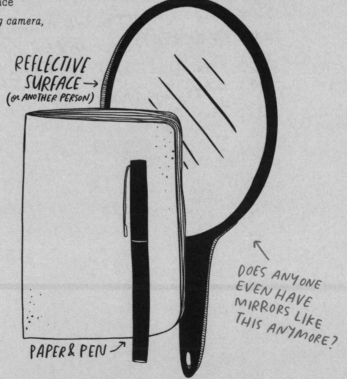

REFLECTIVE
SURFACE →
(or ANOTHER PERSON)

PAPER & PEN →

↖
DOES ANYONE
EVEN HAVE
MIRRORS LIKE
THIS ANYMORE?

The Practice

OR ANOTHER BEING

1. Situate yourself in front of a mirror (or front-facing camera) with a pen and paper.

2. Take a deep breath and look yourself in the eye.

TAKE YOUR TIME HERE

3. After acquainting yourself with your reflection, take your pen in hand, focus your eye on one specific part of your face, and begin to draw yourself <u>in one continuous line</u>. Let your eye trace the lines of your face, focusing on the edges or contours. Trust your hand to follow along.

4. Try to keep your pen and gaze in sync. <u>Do not look at your paper or lift your pen until you have</u> completed your drawing.

— TRY YOUR BEST! IT'S HARD TO RESIST

5. When you are finished, jot down whatever you are thinking or feeling at that moment. This will be the title of your portrait.

DON'T OVERTHINK IT

TRY THIS!

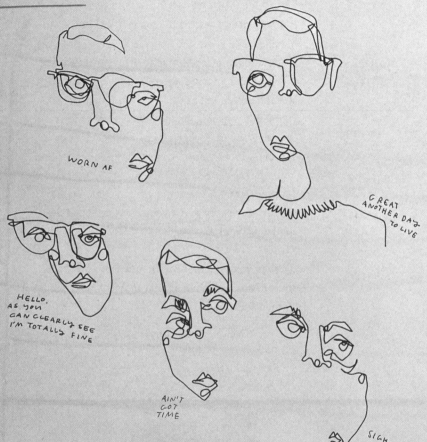

WORN AF

GREAT
ANOTHER DAY
TO LIVE

HELLO.
AS YOU
CAN CLEARLY SEE
I'M TOTALLY FINE

AIN'T
GOT
TIME

SIGH

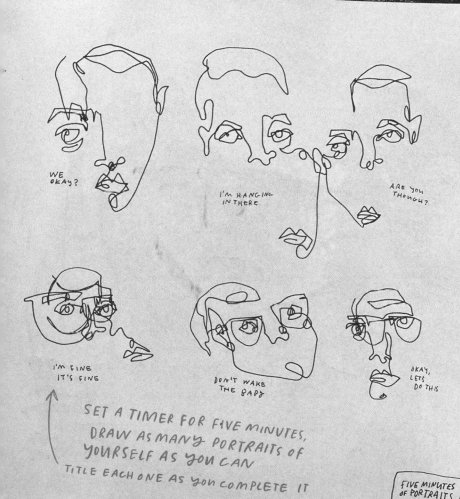

WE
OKAY?

I'M HANGING
IN THERE.

ARE YOU
THOUGH?

I'M FINE
IT'S FINE

DON'T WAKE
THE BABY

OKAY,
LETS
DO THIS

SET A TIMER FOR FIVE MINUTES,
DRAW AS MANY PORTRAITS OF
YOURSELF AS YOU CAN
TITLE EACH ONE AS YOU COMPLETE IT

FIVE MINUTES
OF PORTRAITS

2/11
2021

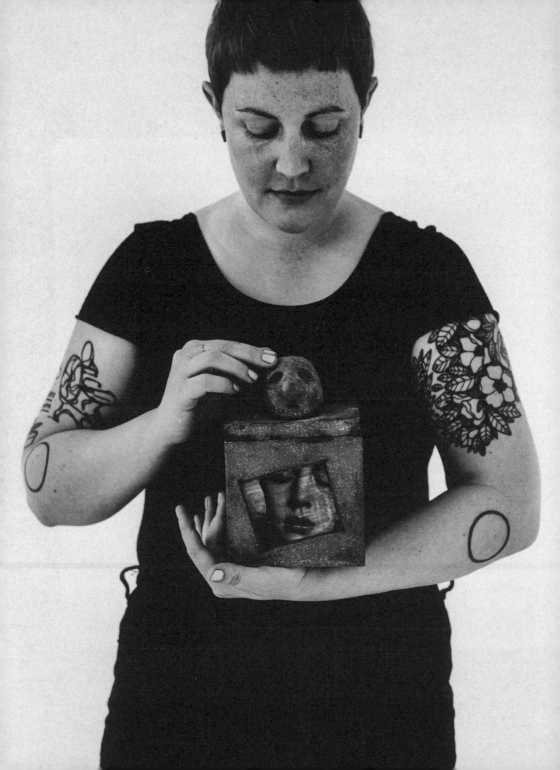

SELF-PORTRAITURE

I am of the persuasion that *almost all* art-making is self-reflective. Every little thing you consume, delight in, capture, produce, share, or pause to wonder at; it's all a mirror back to you. But since we need a place to start, let's define a self-portraiture as a photograph you take of yourself. Okay? Here we might ask, what's the difference between a self-portrait and a selfie? Some days I argue they're the same, others I dance with separating them. You can decide for yourself.

Tools

1. Camera
2. Your body

ANY KIND OF
CAMERA WILL DO:
FILM, INSTANT,
DIGITAL, or YOUR
TRUSTY PHONE!

It feels wrong to tell you how to take a self-portrait. It's the most intimate form of art-making, in my opinion. What I want most for you is to feel unburdened by prompts or ideas. For you to simply be with yourself and capture what you find there. Taking portraits of myself is a spiritual practice. Evidence of my existence, power over my image and my body, and an acknowledgment of all that I hold within me.

HOPE IT WILL BE FOR YOU TOO

HERE ARE SOME PROMPTS, IF THAT FEELS USEFUL TO YOU

PLAY! PLAY! PLAY! PLAY! PLAY! PLAY!

What positions feel good to you? What kind of light do you like? What is it like to be in charge of how you are represented? You are your own audience. What does that feel like? How do you want to be seen? What is it to be in your body? What form is gender taking for you today? What shapes can you make with the form of your body? What objects feel important to you? Can you integrate them into your portrait? How much of your body needs be in the frame for it to be a self-portrait? What's the difference between a selfie and a self-portrait? Where do they coexist? Why do we call one art and not the other? What are you trying to capture in each? Does it matter?

MAKE IT CEREMONY

Make it a ceremony, spend time alone, get acquainted with yourself. Take a hot shower or bath, consider getting friendly with your self, engage in your favorite forms of self-grooming, and adorn yourself in whatever manner makes you feel the most THE MOST. Ya feel me?

DON'T MAKE A FUSS

Make a practice of not making a fuss. If you feel flustered, that's okay. Let yourself be that way. Let it be as messy, frenetic, and obsessive as you feel. The only wrong way to do this is to overthink yourself out of it.

CAPTURE EMOTION

Take a photo when you feel happy, sad, lonely, angry, excited, anxious, etc. How does it feel to have stills of your face from various states of being? Did the act of taking a self-portrait relieve or intensify your emotions?

MAKE A COLLECTION

Try taking a photo of yourself at the same time every day, or in the same position or place. Build a collection based on time, space, posture, or another constant to give yourself gentle structure.

| the making |

PLAY WITH MIRRORS, YOUR PHONE, DISPOSABLE CAMERA, INSTAX (Polaroid), DSLR, or ANY OTHER MEANS OF REPRODUCING YOUR LIKENESS.

LET IT BE
LIGHT, LET IT
BE FUN!

MANIFESTOS

A manifesto is a personal guide. A reference,
directive, and reminder. A line in the sand and
flag held high. It is an extension of your body
and should be written somatically.

Manifestos take many forms. Yours might look
like a poem or a list. Perhaps it's just a few short
lines that capture your values, or maybe it goes
on for pages.

YOU ARE
IN THE INTOX...
YOUR BODY LEAR...
ENDLESS CAPACIT...
PASSION FLOWING T...
DELIGHT YOU AND FR...
OTHERS. TRY AND FR...
DO NOT BECOME
IDENTITY. STAND TALL. L...
YOUR WORTH IS INHER...
SMALL FOR THE COMFOR... OF OTHERS. DO
EXPAND. FILL YOUR LUNGS WITH AIR. AND GROW.
YOU BODY WITH FOOD. DO NOT DENY YOU...
SELF NURISHMENT. DO NOT BE SILENCED. DO
NOT SHRINK, DO NOT CONFORM. YOU ARE A
INDOMITABLE. A FORMIDABLE FORCE.
STARE AT YOURSELF. LEARN YOUR BODY.
BE THRILD AT THE SIGHT OF FLAWS.
THEY ARE A STURDY FINGER IN THE FACE
OF PATRIARCHY. OWN THEM. BECOME THEM.
THRILL YOURSELF. DO NOT STOP AT
SATISFACTION. PURSUE ECSTASY.
YOU ARE A FUCKING GODDESS.
AND I LOVE YOU.

THIS IS THE FIRST
MANIFESTO I EVER WROTE –
I STARTED BY WRITING ALL
THE MESSAGES I RECEIVED AS
A CHILD AND TEEN.
THEN I WHITEWASHED OVER
IT AND REWROTE THE TRUTH
OF MY EXISTENCE.

Tools

1. Any apparatus for recording words
pen and paper, computer, typewriter, your notes app,
audio recorder, or any other means of capturing
your beliefs, desires, and values with language

2. Time and space for self-reflection

A personal manifesto is a living, breathing document, morphing and evolving just like you do. As such, you don't have to worry about it being perfect.

It is forever a rough draft.

Write as though it is already done. Use declarative sentences. Be direct. Or maybe that isn't your style, in which case be poetic, dramatic, or flowery. The only rule is that there aren't any rules. (Unless you need them—and then you should create a framework for yourself.) ← *TRUST YOUR OWN PROCESS*

Write in full sentences and paragraphs or allow yourself to distort and reframe the language you use. Write freely. Do not censor yourself. See what comes out of the depths within you. Then arrange your words in any form that makes the most sense. These are the phrases and fragments you will stretch to guide your consciousness forward.

ALLOW YOURSELF TO BE SURPRISED!

Two of my favorite artists, Marina Abramović and Sister Corita Kent, wrote different but equally brillant manifestos about how to be an artist. I love seeing the various ways folks order their values and beliefs. It's like getting a copy of the map they use to orient their lives within this weird, wild, wonderful world. Look for manifestos written by your favorite humans, past or present. What can you learn from/about them based on the guidelines they've set out for themselves? What kinds of rules, boundaries, framework, guides, etc., do you want to declare for yourself?

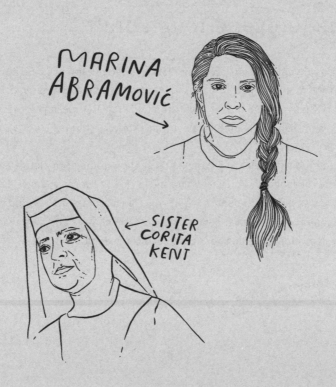

MARINA ABRAMOVIĆ

SISTER CORITA KENT

LISA CONGDON

Speaking of values, Lisa Congdon co-created a stunning deck of cards with Andreea Niculescu, exploring seventy-eight different values. It's an amazing resource for establishing what matters most to you. This is a brilliant place to start your manifesto-writing journey. Try writing a manifesto from your core values, then reference it when you're faced with decisions, big and small. I like doing this quarterly, so I can get super specfic about what matters to me in that season. You can write as many manifestos as you want for yourself. Try ones that apply just to right now, or a certain facet of your life, as well as broad, overarching guidelines that might last a lifetime. In my opinion, the most important part is that it remains malleable and adaptive.

Check in often to make sure your actions and values are in alignment. It's a sticky feeling to be operating outside of the things that matter to you. Are you experiencing a dissonance of theory versus practice in your life? I'd first check to make sure the beliefs and values you're holding on to are actually ones you want to carry. Then see how you can shift your life to better harmonize with your values.

INTUITIVELY RESPOND TO THESE PROMPTS →

THEN ASK YOURSELF WHY: WHY DOES THIS MATTER, AND WHY IS THAT? AND WHY, AND WHY, AND WHY...

Remember the mindmapping flow on page 58? Reference it as you respond to these prompts. I recommend long, messy lists, writing intuitively, and using your whole body when you can. Hang sheets of paper on the wall and use a thick Sharpie so you can write big and bold. Allow yourself to take up space with your language and body.

WHAT DO YOU WANT TO ATTRACT?

WHAT DO YOU FANTASIZE ABOUT?

WHAT GUIDES YOUR BELIEFS? WHERE DID THEY COME FROM?

WHAT EXISTS IN the TENSION BETWEEN?

WHAT ARE YOU RUNNING TOWARD?

WHAT MAKES YOU ANGRY?

WHAT DO YOU RUN FROM?

WHAT DO YOU WANT TO REPEL?

FOLD DOWN A SCRAP OF PAPER INTO
a ZINE. SCRIBBLE YOUR FEELINGS
INTO IT, LET THE WEIGHT OF BEING ALIVE
IN THIS WORLD REST ON THE PAGE.
TAKE A PHOTO OF THE SKY & REMEMBER
ALL THAT EXISTS IS THIS VERY MOMENT.
TYPE FURIOUSLY INTO YOUR NOTES
APP INSTEAD OF SENDING AN ANGRY
TEXT. FIND A MIRROR & DRAW
YOURSELF. TURN ON YOUR FAVORITE
MUSIC, SING AT THE TOP OF YOUR
LUNGS. DANCE! WRITE A POEM,
WRITE A LETTER TO YOUR PAST
SELF, FUTURE SELF. WRITE TO
YOUR HEROES, WRITE a MANIFESTO.
MEDITATE, BREATHE, STRETCH,
DRINK a GLASS OF WATER.
MAKE a COLLAGE, COMIC, OR
COLOR AN ENTIRE PAGE WITH
ONE CRAYON. DRAW YOUR FRIENDS,
TAKE A PHOTO OF YOUR FAVORITE TREE
EVERYDAY FOR A YEAR. SCRATCH
SHAPES INTO THE DIRT WITH a STICK.
WHENEVER YOU FEEL SOMETHING,
PAUSE TO MAKE SOMETHING, anything!

I WILL MAKE

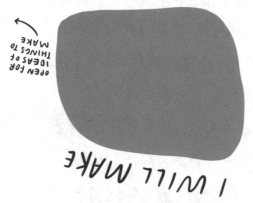

OPEN FOR IDEAS OF THINGS TO MAKE →

AS A WAY TO

- SUSTAIN (NURTURE/PROLONG)
- CHANNEL (DIRECT/TRANSMIT)
- SHIFT (ALTER/CONVERT)

MY FEELING(S) AND FIND A STEADY PLACE WITHIN MYSELF

I AM FEELING

NAME YOUR FEELING OR FEELINGS

IT HAS TAKEN UP RESIDENCE IN MY

PART OR PARTS OF YOUR BODY

ON THE SPECTRUM of HIGH to LOW, MY ENERGY/MOOD IS

MELANCHOLIA DEPRESSION NUMB

FRENETIC ANXIOUS BUZZING

HERE IS A LITTLE BIT OF PAPER TO KEEP IN YOUR POCKET OR DESK FOR MOMENTS WHEN YOU'RE HAVING A BIG FEEL

FOR MORE YOU CAN FOLLOW @CAITLINHASFEELS

SO YOU'RE HAVING a FEELING

NOW WHAT?

MY DARLINGS,

YOUR WORK DOESN'T HAVE TO BE
GOOD OR MAKE YOU ANY MONEY.

YOU NEED ONLY TO FEEL DEEPLY
AND GIVE IT FORM.

YOUR MARKS SERVE AS EVIDENCE
THAT YOU WERE HERE, ALIVE, AND
IN THE WORLD. LET THE PROCESS
SOFTEN YOU;

FEEL SOMETHING,
MAKE SOMETHING.
RINSE & REPEAT.

I HOPE YOU CREATE LOTS OF PERFECTLY
UGLY, TERRIBLE, BEAUTIFUL THINGS.

all MY LOVE,
CAITLIN

P.S. TEAR OUT THIS TINY GUIDE
TO KEEP HANDY FOR WHEN
YOU'RE HAVING A FEEL

A few incomplete words about the folks who have championed me and my work.

SARA NEVILLE

My god. There aren't words. You have been unrelenting in your care of me and this book. I owe you more than I even know. How are you real?! Thank you, thank you, thank you. Let's never stop making things together, okay?

DANIELLE DESCHENES

Thank you for carrying these pages over the finish line, you saved me from myself. Truly.

LUISA FRANCAVILLA, JOYCE WONG, AND CHLOE ARYEH

Thanks for spell checking my ass and doing all the mystical, behind the scenes magic that gets books onto shelves and bedside tables. Y'all are the real deal.

LAURA LEE MATTINGLY

Thank you for seeing me and the possibility of my ideas. For advocating and cheering. You're the first pick on my team, now and always.

KAPLAN TRUDO, IAN KING, AND UNHYE MYONG

My kindreds, my loves. Thank you for being with me through the many stages of doubt, triumph, and terror while making this book, as well as every other creative endeavor I've pursued. If I'm ever brave or kind or honest, it's because you've taught me how.

HAL & DIANA METZ

For giving me a childhood filled with art supplies and trees to climb. Thanks for cheering me on even when you don't understand or agree with me. I love you forever and always.

KIRSTEN METZLIMING

For taking every panicked call/frantic text when I couldn't find the word I was looking for. How is your vocabulary so good?! You're my best and favorite sounding board. I love you, Pookie.

SCOTT & TRACY GILLILAN

For loving the bean so well while I labored over these pages. For believing in my work. For my studio, my gosh. What a gift.

ANDREW GILLILAN

My quiet champion. Sometimes I forget how integral you are to my practice because of how seamlessly you fill in the gaps while being completely unaffected by my success or failure. You are the anchor that steadies my sail. Thank you, my love.

CHARLIE METZ-GILLILAN

You were just a whisper inside me when I pitched this book and now you'll be nearly three years old when these words come into the world. This journey has been slowed and perfected by your presence. I couldn't imagine it any other way. I love you, sweet bean.